THE
TRIAL
OF
JOB

Orthodox Christian Reflections on
The Book of Job

by Patrick Henry Reardon

Conciliar Press
Ben Lomond, California

THE TRIAL OF JOB:
Orthodox Christian Reflections on the Book of Job
© Copyright 2005 by Patrick Henry Reardon

All Rights Reserved

Published by   Conciliar Press
                    P.O. Box 76
                    Ben Lomond, California 95005-0076

Printed in the United States of America

ISBN 1-888212-72-1

Manufactured under the direction of Double Eagle Industries.
For manufacturing details, call 888-824-4344

I presume on the charity of the parishioners
of All Saints' Orthodox Church in Chicago
to accept, from their unworthy pastor,
the dedication of this humble work

CONTENTS

INTRODUCTION
੩੧

"YOU HAVE HEARD OF THE PERSEVERANCE OF JOB," wrote St. James, "and seen the end *intended by* the Lord—that the Lord is very compassionate and merciful" (James 5:11).

It is useful to begin this study of Job with a glance at James, I think, not only because James is the only New Testament writer to mention Job explicitly, but also because he provides the traditional Christian approach to Job—namely, the theme of the just man who is tried in his faith.

In this respect, it is worth citing the immediate context of that passage in James: "My brethren, take the prophets, who spoke in the name of the Lord, as an example of suffering and patience. Indeed, we count them blessed [*makarizomen*] who endure [*hypomeinantes*]" (5:10–11). It is precisely at this point that James refers to Job, the only figure he mentions by name in his reference to "the prophets."

In this text, moreover, James is resuming a theme he introduced earlier in his epistle, the blessedness of the man who is put to the trial: "Blessed [*makarios*] *is* the man who endures [*hypomenei*] temptation; for when he has been approved, he will receive the crown of life which the Lord has promised to those who love Him" (1:12). Job appears, then, as James' example of the "blessed man" who endured.

Following the lead of James, Christians have long admired this figure they called "the great Job—*ho megas Iob*" (Hippolytus of Rome, *Ad Iudaios* 4.8). Especially have they revered Job as the loyal, longsuffering, godly man put to trial in his faith. Thus, prior to the year 100, Clement of Rome listed him, under this aspect, between Abraham and Moses (*First Clement* 17.2). This was exactly the perspective of Clement of Alexandria, who paired Job, in this same respect, with the prophet Daniel (*Stromateis* 2.20). Basil the Great (*Letters* 2) and Ambrose of Milan (*De Officiis* 24.113–114) coupled Job with the patiently enduring Joseph. Cyril of Jerusalem, for his part, included this longsufferer in a more substantial list of "righteous men and prophets" (*Catechetical Lectures* 16.27).

Christians have also given attention to the fact that Job's sufferings were occasioned by Satan. That is to say, his fight was not against flesh and blood, but against "the rulers of the darkness of this age." In this story, wrote Gregory the Theologian, we behold a contest between the virtue of Job and the envy of the devil (*Orationes* 21.18). For John Chrysostom, the fact that Satan was in arms against Job was the supreme testimony in his favor (*Homilies on Romans* 15).

Such is the general approach to Job preferred in the Christian Church, exemplified in the troparion that we annually chant on his feast day, May 6: "When the enemy of the just man beheld the treasures of Job's virtues, he sought to destroy them. He attacked his body but could not touch his spirit, for his pure soul was ready and strong. As for ourselves, the enemy has stripped and chained us. Wherefore, O Savior, be on our side, protect us from the devil, and save us."

We must not think, however, that the Church's interest in the Book of Job is only moral. A yet deeper sense of the book is discerned in the practice of the Church to read Job during Holy Week, the very season of our Lord's suffering and death. This ancient liturgical custom, to which Ambrose testified at Milan in the fourth century (*Letters* 20.14), stands in testimony to the Church's regard of patient Job as a figure and type of Jesus, supremely the Just Man suffering and sorely tried. Job is, wrote Gregory the Great, "a type of the Redeemer" (*Moralia in Iob*, Preface).

Job's Character & the Structure of the Book

In the text with which I began, St. James sends us to the "end intended by the Lord" (*to telos Kyriou*) in the Book of Job, and I will argue in this study that that ending in chapter 42 is not only the resolution of the drama, but also the key to Job's character. This key, let me here suggest, commences with the Lord's word to Eliphaz the Temanite, who represents all of Job's comforters: "'Now therefore, take for yourselves seven bulls and seven rams, go to My servant Job, and offer up for yourselves a burnt offering; and My servant Job shall pray for you. For I will accept him, lest I deal with you *according to your* folly; because you have not spoken of Me *what is* right, as My servant Job *has*.' So Eliphaz the Temanite and Bildad the Shuhite *and* Zophar the Naamathite went and did as the LORD commanded them; for the LORD had accepted Job. And the LORD restored Job's losses when he prayed for his friends.

Indeed the LORD gave Job twice as much as he had before" (Job 42:8–10). In this passage near the very end of the book, Job appears preeminently as an effective petitioner on behalf of his friends. These men are restored to God's favor by Job's praying for them, and Job himself recovers *by* his praying for them. The story of Job is thus interpreted through the singular mystery of intercessory prayer.

Moreover, this explanation of Job was not lost on those familiar with the story. For example, the Prophet Ezekiel, remembering Job's prayer more than his patience, listed him with Noah and Daniel, all three of whom he took to be men endowed with singular powers of intercession before the Most High (Ezekiel 14:14–20).

This theme of Job's intercessory prayer appears almost immediately at the beginning of the book, thus binding the first chapter to the last. Indeed, we learn of Job's intercession almost before we discover anything else about him. Concerned for the welfare of his ten children, we are told, Job "would rise early in the morning and offer burnt offerings *according to* the number of them all" (Job 1:5). Let me suggest that between Job's intercessions at the beginning and the end of the book, we may regard chapters 2 through 37 as a kind of Satanic distraction to Job's life of prayer.

About halfway through the book, Job's final prayer is prophesied by Eliphaz in a verse of great irony: "You will make your prayer to Him, / He will hear you, / And you will pay your vows" (22:27). To show that this prophecy has been fulfilled, it is to Eliphaz that God directs His rebuke and command at the end of the story (42:7–8). Job's wisdom, then, has to do with his prayer for those he loves.

Job himself is given three lifetimes, as it were. There is the central story of his trial, framed between a before and an after, with the period of his trial being the central dividing point of his allotted days. This structure is essential to the whole account. Without its beginning and its end, the Book of Job would be a completely different work. Indeed, I think it would be an unintelligible work. (For this reason I mention certain modern critical theories, which regard the beginning and end of Job as later additions to the book, only in order to hold them in scorn.)

It is useful to compare the book's beginning and its end. Doing so, we discern that Job lives 140 years, exactly twice the normal span of a man's life (see Psalm 89[90]:10). Each of his first seven sons and three daughters is *replaced* at the end of the story, and all of his original livestock is exactly *doubled* (Job 1:3; 42:12). St. Gregory the Great, in his very long commentary on Job (*Moralia in Iob*), draws attention to the significance of the doubling of Job's blessings in the final chapter. For Gregory this doubling signifies the eternal reward of those who, like Job, serve God in the patience of their souls.

Job & the Wisdom Traditions of the Bible

Properly to place the Book of Job in the context of the Sacred Canon, it will be useful to consider how it is related to those other biblical works that we call wisdom books.

The Bible has two major kinds of wisdom books. The somewhat larger group, represented chiefly by the Books of Proverbs and Sirach (Ecclesiasticus), may be described as "traditional," in the sense that the emphasis in these books falls on such moral themes as are needed for the transmission of a living culture. These themes include fidelity to inherited standards, respect for the teachings of parents and elders, adherence to historical legacies, and so forth. Accordingly, the tone in these books is consistently conservative.

A living culture, after all, is necessarily conservative. It does not start with philosophical speculation. It begins, rather, with the basic moral requirements for survival. One of these requirements is common, simple prudence, identified by Plato as one of the four essential virtues of the moral life (the other three being justice, self-restraint, and fortitude). This first kind of wisdom recognized in the Bible, the wisdom taught in the Book of Proverbs, is based on practical prudence. This is the kind of wisdom properly and primarily handed down in families.

Israel started, we know, as a family and grew from a family to a nation. As Israel became a full political entity at the Exodus, there emerged the need to incorporate that ancient familial trait, practical prudence, into its public and official policies. This need became especially acute with the founding of the monarchy near the end of the eleventh century before Christ. At that time it became necessary to advance intelligent men to positions of national leadership, and even to train young men for such roles. As Israel endeavored to create a geopolitical place for itself near the western end of the Fertile Crescent, selectmen were educated in the arts of diplomacy, finance, and international trade.

Alongside this sophisticated cultivation of political prudence, Israel's search for wisdom was also preserved in the folk traditions of its nongoverning citizens, especially the farmers, craftsmen, and local merchants. These folk traditions formed the living context of Israel's earliest quest for wisdom.

With respect to style, this first kind of wisdom literature is dominated by short, pithy sayings, easily memorized from childhood—that is, proverbs. The recommended wisdom is always of a practical kind, having to do with sobriety of judgment, prudence in one's business affairs and matters of state, personal discipline in the use of one's time, money, and other resources, strict marital fidelity and the consequent joys of home and family. (Indeed, all of the four moral virtues of Plato—prudence, justice, self-restraint, and fortitude—are abundantly contained in the Book of Proverbs.)

This first kind of biblical wisdom is what may be called "tried and true." Proved repeatedly in the experience of previous generations, it is safe and sane. It quietly presumes that the big speculative questions, if there really were any, have all been answered and taken care of.

Therefore, this type of wisdom does not, generally speaking, raise theoretical reflections about the meaning and purpose of life. It contains nothing suggestive of the "cutting edge" of new ideas that might distract from the serious business of getting on with a good, virtuous life. Although this literature may occasionally note some ironical feature of destiny, it does not directly address such large and thorny concerns. It tends to ask rather "how" a person should live than "why" he should do so. If life presents problems, this wisdom says, just keep the commandments, respect the tradition handed down from your parents, work hard, be careful, don't be a scoffer, and everything will turn out just fine.

Besides this traditional, conservative kind, however, there is a second sort of wisdom literature in the Bible, represented by the Books of Ecclesiastes (Qoheleth) and Job. These books, not content simply to repeat Israel's inherited answers, demonstrate a more probing and "problematic" purpose. They make a point of addressing difficult and thorny questions about the meaning of human existence itself. They address such difficult questions as how to reconcile the existence of evil and suffering with the existence of an all-good, all-wise, and almighty God.

This second kind of literature is most certainly not conservative. It tends, rather, to be bold. Its anxious voice pushes toward the outer limits of speculative reflection on the human problems of suffering, futility, and frustration. For example, unlike the Book of Proverbs, which regards life as a task to be gotten through successfully, Ecclesiastes repeatedly laments that "all is vanity." The author of Ecclesiastes, facing frustration and even a sense of despair throughout all of existence, seems perpetually on the brink of discouragement and despondency, sentiments quite alien to the Books of Ecclesiasticus and Proverbs.

Like Ecclesiastes, Job is also a discomforting book, for it deals with a very thorny question: the suffering of those who do not deserve to suffer. Job is portrayed as an eminently just man. He has fulfilled all of his responsibilities and more. He has offended in nothing.

Indeed, Job has lived as the very embodiment of the ideals set forth in the Book of Proverbs. He has amply displayed all the virtues taught in that source: prudence, justice, self-restraint, and fortitude. Job's whole life, prior to the crisis described in the book named after him, may be called an illustration of the ideals contained in Proverbs.

Well could Job expect, then, the happiness that the Book of Proverbs confidently promises to those who adhere to the dictates of Israel's traditional wisdom. After all, one of the most salient ideas in that book is its joining of goodness to good fortune. That is to say, good things happen to good people.

Job, however, is visited with bad fortune. Instead of continued blessings, he is visited with all manner of evil, disgrace, humiliation, and suffering. Why? Job wants to know.

At this point Job is visited by his three "comforters," who bring him anything but comfort. These gentlemen, as we shall see in our comments on the book, become the spokesmen for various theories that endeavor to *explain* Job's problem. One of these men especially, Eliphaz the Temanite, becomes the voice of the older tradition of wisdom, that of the Book of Proverbs.

Job, however, finds no comfort, no satisfaction, in the various attempts made to explain his sufferings. This is the source of his moral dilemma, which is the dominant theme of the book's long central section.

In the course of the work various possible answers to Job's questions are tried, weighed, and mostly found wanting. For this reason the Book of Job may be described, like the Book of Ecclesiastes, as speculative. The various answers advanced are tentative rather than definitive. Its mental map is not entirely filled in. Its thesis is more probed than proved.

The book ends on the note of faith in God but, like Ecclesiastes, it permits the speculative thought of the believer to explore the darker, more mysterious dimensions of that faith.

Of special importance is God's direct revelation of Himself to Job in the final chapter. All through the book, Job has been insisting on his own righteousness. He repeats the theme over and over, in the face of the protestations of his unhelpful friends. At the end, however, God shows something of Himself to Job's inner vision, and no longer is our questioner able with confidence to call himself a righteous man. On the contrary, he falls down in humility and self-contempt: "I have heard of You by the hearing of the ear, / But now my eye sees You. / Therefore, I abhor *myself*, / And repent in dust and ashes" (42:5–6).

This is the whole Bible's definitive word, in fact, about the prospects of human righteousness: that it won't work. One finds salvation only in faith, repentance, a healthy contempt of self, and a saving trust in God's fidelity to His promises. One observes this same attitude repeatedly throughout the epistles of Paul the Apostle.

Job, the Righteous Pagan
It has long been noted that Israel's wisdom literature is the place where the Old Testament most readily touches the religious experience and aspirations of mankind in general, and this observation seems especially pertinent with respect to Job. He is not, after all, a Jew. Whether or not Job is to be identified as a descendent of Esau (according to the Peshitta and some manuscripts of the LXX), he is most certainly portrayed as a Gentile. John Chrysostom drew particular attention to this fact, linking Job with other righteous pagans like Melchizedek the priest-king and Cornelius the centurion (*Homilies on Romans* 5).

It is not surprising, therefore, that the Book of Job has often been likened to other ancient works that treat of the undeserved sufferings of just men. One of these works, the meditation of a despondent Egyptian of the early second millennium before Christ, debates the option of suicide to escape an unbearable life. Another, this one from Mesopotamia, begins "I will praise the Lord of wisdom." It is the prayer of a man who has recently recovered from a terrible illness and now seeks to know its cause. The character in this poem has sometimes been called, in fact, a "Babylonian Job." Such texts from Egypt and the Middle East, and even India, are numerous.

More familiar to most readers, perhaps, are the possible parallels to Job from classical Greek literature, where fate (*moira*) causes men to suffer in order to preclude proud rebellion (*hybris*) from their hearts. The Greek tragedies come to mind in respect to Job, perhaps none more than the *Prometheus Bound* of Aeschylus. Like the Book of Job itself, this one includes a lengthy dialogue, in which Oceanus and the nymphs counsel Prometheus to confess his offense against Zeus in order to be set free from the rock to which he is chained in punishment for stealing the gift of fire.

These examples are mentioned here, not because I think them historically related to the Book of Job, but because they do, in fact, touch on certain common themes. In respect to this point, however, it is important to observe that the God in the Book of Job is the LORD, the God of the Jews. As I will remark in the commentary itself, this is the Name by which He is called in both the opening and ending chapters of the book, even though the various characters throughout the book, none of them Jews, normally speak simply of "God."

The Present Commentary

What I have written here is not meant to be a full theological treatment of the Book of Job. Such commentaries, in fact, have already been written. I am thinking of the great commentaries of Hesychius of Jerusalem, John Chrysostom, and especially Gregory the Great, whose outstanding works I hesitate even to mention in so modest a book as this. In particular, I cannot sufficiently recommend the distillation of those rich, ancient commentaries compiled in Johanna Manley's magisterial *Wisdom, Let Us Attend: Job, the Fathers, and the Old Testament* (Menlo Park, California: Monastery Books, 1997).

My aspirations in the present work are appropriately more modest. This is a plain book for plain readers. Nowhere in these pages will anyone discover the faintest trace of scholarship. These are just unembellished reflections composed by a simple parish priest who has in mind, as readers, the sorts of people that it is his blessing to pastor here in Chicago. Indeed, some of these pages first appeared in the Old Testament sermons that I deliver every Wednesday and Saturday evening at Vespers. Other parts first saw light in the "Daily Reflections" that I post to the website of *Touchstone* (www. touchstonemag.com/frpat.html).

I forswear, consequently, the sorts of technical problems that scholars must face. I eschew, for instance, all efforts to ascribe author-ship or dating to the Book of Job. In respect to this last point, I hope it will suffice to say that I believe it to be late, post-exilic. My reasons for this opinion are two and simple. First, if Job were an early book, it arguably would have been included among the prophetic books, not the *Ketubim*. After all, in Christian literature Job is very often called a prophet, and there is nothing intrinsic to the book, I think, to preclude it from the prophetic books.

Second, the demonic figure in the first two chapters, Satan, seems to have come to Israel's attention during the Persian period, for he was a demon very well known among the disciples of Zoroaster. This too would suggest the Persian period as the time of Job's composition. How-ever, this does not mean that the story of Job was unknown before the writing of the book. Indeed, the mention of Job himself by Ezekiel during the Captivity indicates the very opposite. Let me say, nonethe-less, that I make all such comments by way of suggestion only. No part of the present work will stand or fall with a particular dating of Job.

As part of my studied neglect of scholarship in these pages, I will also avoid entirely the vast, complex problems presented by the multi-faceted textual history of the Book of Job. Even though the reflections that follow are generally based on the traditional Hebrew text of the book (with consultation of the LXX and Vulgate), I hope I have written a commentary that can be profitably read along with *any* translation of Job.

PHR
January 27, 2005
The Feast of the Translation of the Relics of St. John Chrysostom

JOB 1

༈

THE BOOK OF JOB BEGINS LIKE THE BOOK OF PSALMS, by describing "the blessings of a man" (*'ashrei ha'ish*). "A man there was, in the land of Uz," it commences, *'ish haya b'erets 'uts*. This parallel between Job and Psalms is significant. In the Hebrew text of Holy Scripture, though not in the Septuagint (LXX), the Books of Psalms and Job stand in immediate sequence. In the Greek and Latin Bibles, the Book of Job serves as a kind of transition from the narrative books (Joshua through Esther) to the wisdom literature (Psalms through Ecclesiasticus). Job is at once a work of narrative and a work of sapient reflection; it is both history and (for want of a better term) philosophy.

This sequence, moreover, prompts comparative reflection on the beginnings of both Job and Psalms. The first chapter of Job describes him, in fact, as the embodiment of the ideals held out in the first psalm. Job "walks not in the counsel of the ungodly, / Nor stands in the path of sinners, / Nor sits in the seat of the scornful." On the contrary, he is "like a tree planted by the rivers of water, / That brings forth its fruit in its season, / Whose leaf also shall not wither; / And whatever he does shall prosper."

Whereas the "man" in the first psalm is clearly a Jew, whose "delight *is* in the law of the LORD," Job is only a man—any just man, anywhere. St. John Chrysostom drew special attention to the fact that Job is only a man, not a Jew. That is to say, Job does not enjoy the benefits of the revelation made to God's chosen people. The only revelation known to Job is that which is accorded to all men, namely, that God "is, and *that* He is a rewarder of those who diligently seek Him" (Hebrews 11:6).

The first verse of Job introduces the narrative prologue (1:1—2:13) preceding the lengthy and complicated dialogue that forms the long central core of the book. This prologue contains six scenes:

    (1) an account of Job's life and prosperity in 1:1–5;

    (2) the first discussion in heaven in 1:6–12;

    (3) Job's loss of his children and possessions in 1:13–22;

    (4) the second discussion in heaven in 2:1–7;

(5) Job's affliction of the flesh in 2:7–10;
(6) the arrival of Job's three friends in 2:11–13.

Chapter 1, then, contains the first three of these six scenes.

In the first scene (1:1–5) Job is called a devout man who feared God, a man who "shunned evil." He thus enjoyed the prosperity promised to such folk in Israel's wisdom literature. As we have reflected in our introduction to this book, Job is the very embodiment of the prosperous just man held up as a model in the Book of Proverbs.

The second scene (1:6–12) describes the first discussion between God and "*the Satan*," "the Adversary." Satan, the name of the "accuser of our brethren, who accused them . . . day and night" (Revelation 12:9–10), was also known to the Prophet Zechariah (3:1–4). The LXX identifies Job's tempter as "the Slanderer" (*ho Diabolos*, whence the English derivative "devil"). Satan and "the devil" are identified in Matthew 4:8–10 and elsewhere in the New Testament.

According to the Hebrew text of Job, Satan is numbered among the "sons of God," an expression that the LXX understands as a reference to the angels. The Christian Church, following the lead of such passages as Matthew 25:41 ("the devil and his angels"), understands Satan to be the leader of the fallen angels.

Satan's argument against Job is simple and plausible: If a just man is so richly blest in his uprightness, who is to say that this just man is really so loyal to God? May it not be the case that the just man is simply taking good care of his own interest? Let the alleged just man, then, be put to the test.

Indeed, ever since the first man who lived in prosperity, Adam in the Garden, this demonic Adversary has been endeavoring to put man to the test. The greatest trial of Job will come in the consideration of his own mortality, which is the sad inheritance he has received from Adam. We must not lose sight of Job's antithesis to Adam. Job's faithful service to God in this book stands in sharp relief against the disobedience of Adam, which brought death into the world.

In this second scene (1:6–12), the discussion between God and Satan, we do well to observe three things: First, the trial of Job will be like that of Abraham, who also enjoyed the rich blessings of a just man. Indeed, Job appears as a sort of Gentile Abraham. As St. Hesychius of Jerusalem remarked in his homilies on Job back in the fifth century, we should not wander too far from the trial of Abraham in Genesis 22 when we consider the trials of Job.

Second, God is an optimist (for want of a better word), in the sense that He has great confidence in Job. In this whole book, God is truly on Job's side. Indeed, God is the *only one* in the story completely on Job's side.

Third, Satan appears as a skeptic and a cynic, persuaded that men act only for selfish motives. That is to say, Satan believes that men are very self-centered, pretty much like Satan himself. Thus, Satan has a rather low view of man. God does not have a low view of man. Not least of the ironies of this book, in fact, is the great confidence that God places in Job's fidelity.

When God consents to the testing of His faithful servant, the third scene (1:13–22) describes Job's loss of his children and possessions. Now begins Job's testing. In fact, here begins Job's tragedy.

One does not have to live very long to perceive a certain perverseness about this world, life's strange but innate contrariness that cripples man's stride and corrodes his hope. Indeed, in terms of plain empirical verification, few lines of Holy Scripture seem supported by more and better evidence than St. Paul's testimony that "creation was subjected to futility" (Romans 8:20). This futility is what Job is now going to taste.

This dark sense of things is what the ancient Greeks called "tragedy," a subject the Greeks appear to have pondered more than most. The root word for "tragedy" means "goat" (*tragos*), an animal commonly associated with stubbornness, mischief, aberrance, and even damnation (Matthew 25:32–33). *Tragedy* is the cup that Job will drain before this book is finished.

JOB 2

ॐ

SATAN IS ENDEAVORING TO PROVOKE JOB TO CURSE GOD (1:11), the very sin that Job abhorred and which he had been afraid his children might commit (1:5). In the present chapter Job's own wife will tempt him in this way (2:9). The fourth, fifth, and sixth scenes are the substance of this second chapter.

In the fourth scene (2:1–7), Satan, disappointed at Job's unexpected response to the initial trials, wants to afflict Job in his very flesh, persuaded that this new kind of pain will bring out the worst in him. He predicts that Job, in such a case, will finally curse God (2:5).

Back in Job 1:9, Satan had asked if Job was a just man "for nothing" (*higgam*), meaning "without getting anything out of it." Now God throws this expression back in Satan's face in 2:3—"you moved me to destroy him 'for nothing' [*higgam*]" (NKJV, "without cause"). That is to say, it was not Job that failed the test, but Satan. The reader discerns that God is actually taunting Satan here. As in Psalm 2, the Lord is laughing His enemy to scorn.

Satan, however, now takes his cynicism to a new level. Believing that man is at root selfish, Satan wants Job put to the test in his own flesh, his own person, not simply in his family and possessions. Job's success so far, Satan believes, amounts to nothing more than the experience of survival. So, he contends, let Job's survival be put at risk. Strip him down to his naked existence, deprived of health and reputation, and then see what happens. At that more personal level, the demonic cynic argues, Job will not fear God; he will curse God, rather.

God, ever the optimist with respect to Job, agrees to this new trial, thus introducing the fifth scene (2:7–10), which describes Job's sufferings. These sufferings involve loathsome and unsightly infections that are often mentioned by Job in the later discourses. Treated like a leper, Job goes to sit on the city dump. He becomes a foreshadowing of the Suffering Servant prophesied in the Book of Isaiah: "In His humiliation His justice was taken away, / And who will declare His generation?" (Acts 8:33, quoting Isaiah 53:8 LXX).

Job is dying, and his wife tempts him to curse God before he does so. In short, Job's wife reacts very much as Satan predicted that Job would react.

Indeed, we do perceive a change in Job at this point. If he does not curse God, Job also does not explicitly bless God as he had done in his first affliction (1:21). Instead, he humbly submits to God's will (2:10).

In each case, nonetheless, God's confidence in Job is vindicated. Satan has done his worst to Job, but Job has not succumbed. Like Abraham in Genesis 22, Job has met the trial successfully.

Having done his worst, Satan disappears and is never again mentioned in the book. The rest of the story concerns only God and human beings.

Job's three friends now show up to introduce the sixth and last scene of this prologue (2:11–13), which directly prepares for the long dialogues that make up the book's central section. The three friends are introduced here, precisely because of their important role in the long central section of this book.

Job's friends, we are told, come to "comfort" him. This verb, "to comfort" (niham), is a very important word in the Book of Job. Introduced here at the story's beginning, the expression "comfort" appears several more times, whether in the verb form (7:13; 16:2; 21:34; 29:25) or as the cognate noun (6:10). Whereas Job's friends fail utterly in their efforts to "comfort" him throughout almost the entire book, they do ironically succeed at the end (42:11), after the resolution of Job's conflict by God's revelatory intervention.

A week of silence ensues (2:13), parallel to the week of revelry with which the book began (1:2, 4).

JOB 3

IN THIS THIRD CHAPTER, THE BOOK OF JOB switches from prose to poetry, the style that will be maintained until almost the end of the book.

Job now breaks the week of silence, beginning his lament, a lament that reminds us more of Jeremiah and some of the Psalms, perhaps, than of Israel's wisdom literature. Chapter 3 is, in fact, a prayer that is paralleled in several of the psalms (such as 49, 73, and 139 [LXX 48, 72, 138]). This chapter is simply a lamentation, much like the biblical book that bears that same name.

Like Elijah pursued by Jezebel, Job is weary of life. Indeed, a more detailed comparison between Elijah and Job is amply warranted by the resemblances between this third chapter and 1 Kings 10. The faith of both men is tried in adversity and discouragement.

Job is also to be compared here to the suffering, afflicted Jeremiah. The present chapter resembles the dereliction recorded in such texts as Jeremiah 15 and 20. Like Jeremiah (20:14–18), Job curses (*yeqahlel*) the day he was born (cf. also 1 Kings 19:4; Jonah 4:3, 8; Sirach 23:14). Job does not, however, curse God.

Still, Job has become impatient; he is beginning to experience even God as an enemy. Job's "let there be darkness" (3:4–6) stands in opposition to God's "let there be light" in Creation (Genesis 1:3). In verses 11–12 Job begins the great question "Why?" that will fill so much of the book.

In 3:9 we note the striking image of the "eyelashes of the dawn," referring to the beams of light that radiate from the sun just before its rising.

This very question that Job begins to utter, "Why?" is also heard frequently from the lips of the psalmist. It will in due course be given its definitive sanction by Christ our Lord (Mark 15:34).

In 3:20 the "Why?" becomes more intense and less rhetorical. Theodicy's major problem, how to reconcile innocent suffering with a just, merciful, and almighty God, is now introduced. It is this "Why?" that Job's three friends will endeavor to answer in the discourses of the following chapters. These friends have their own theories on the matter of evil. None of them really suspects the truth of the matter, namely, that God is permitting Job's faith to be tempted.

The Book of Job illustrates what we may call the Bible's "apocalyptic principle," the rule that asserts that "more is happening than seems to be happening." Like Abraham in Genesis 22, Job does not realize that his faith is being tested. Indeed, this is an essential aspect of the book's drama. God knows that Job's faith is being tried, Satan knows it, and we readers know it. None of the other *dramatis personae* in this story, however, has a clue about what is really happening, not even Job. Indeed, especially not Job.

This important interpretive key, the apocalyptic principle, appears in various ways in Holy Scripture, from the "deep sleep" that the Lord casts on the sentinels of Saul (1 Samuel 26:12), to Assyria's being used as the rod of God's wrath (Isaiah 10:5), to the unwitting prophecy uttered by a blasphemous high priest (John 11:49–51). In all such cases there is more happening than seems to be happening. At the Bible's end, the apocalyptic principle forms the very substance of the Book of Revelation. The entire Book of Job is built on this same interpretive principle: More is going on than appears to be going on.

JOB 4

In the course of this book, Job is addressed eight times by his three comforters, an arrangement that permits the first of those speakers, Eliphaz the Temanite, to address him three times. It is probably because he is the eldest of the three men (cf. Job 15:10) that Eliphaz speaks first, and this is surely also the reason that, near the end of the book, God addresses Eliphaz directly as the spokesman of the group (42:7).

A native of Teman, Eliphaz exemplifies the ancient wisdom of Edom (cf. Genesis 36:11), concerning which Jeremiah inquired, "*Is* wisdom no more in Teman? Has counsel perished from the prudent? Has their wisdom vanished?" (Jeremiah 49:7). Eliphaz represents, then, the "wisdom of the south," the great desert region of the Negev and even Arabia, where only the wise can survive.

In his initial response to Job (chapters 4 and 5), Eliphaz appeals to his own personal religious experience. Eliphaz, unlike the other two comforters, is a visionary. He has seen (4:8; 5:3) and heard (4:16) the presence of the divine claims in an experience of such subtlety that he calls it a "whisper" (*shemets*—4:12). This deep sense of the divine absolute, born of Eliphaz's religious experience, forced upon his mind a strongly binding conviction of the divine purity and justice. This profound certainty in his soul became the lens through which Eliphaz interprets the sundry enigmas of life, notably the problem of human suffering.

But this perspective is too narrow, because it does not permit Eliphaz to discern the difference between punishment and trial. For instance, as the Book of Wisdom (11:4–14) commented, both the Egyptians and the Israelites suffered thirst. In the case of the Egyptians, the thirst was a punishment for the drowning of the Hebrew infants in the Nile. In the case of the Israelites, on the other hand, the thirst was a trial of their faith. They both suffered the same torment, but it signified something different in each case. The Egyptians were being punished; the Israelites were being tried.

The shortcoming of Eliphaz, then, consists in his confusion of these things. He and his companions are unable to see that the sufferings of Job do not mean that something is wrong with Job; they mean, on the contrary, that something is *right* with Job. "The friends of Job," wrote St. Gregory the Great, "being unable to distinguish these different kinds of scourges, considered him to be smitten because he was guilty. Hence, they endeavored to vindicate the justice of God for smiting him. They were compelled to blame blessed Job for injustice, unaware that for this reason, in fact, he was stricken—that his scourge might redound to the praise of God's glory."

If we compare Eliphaz to Job's other two comforters, moreover, we observe a gradated but distinct decline in the matter of wisdom. Eliphaz begins the discussion by invoking his own direct spiritual experience, his "vision," his *veda*. As we shall see, however, the second comforter, Bildad the Shuhite, can appeal to no personal experience of his own, but only to the experience of his elders, so what was a true insight in the case of Eliphaz declines to only an inherited theory in the case of Bildad. Living mystical insight becomes merely an inherited moral belief. True vision declines into theoretical dogma.

The same line of decline progresses further in the case of Job's third comforter, because Zophar the Naamathite, unlike Bildad, is unable to invoke even the tradition of his elders. We shall see that Zophar is familiar with neither the living experience of Eliphaz nor the inherited learning of Bildad; his is simply the voice of established prejudice. That is the line of declination: real vision, accepted teaching, blind prejudice.

In these three men, then, we watch an insight decline into a theory, and then the theory harden into a settled, unexamined opinion. Thus do the voices raised against Job throughout this book become ever less persuasive or even morally serious.

As they individually address Job, moreover, each of these men seems progressively less assured of his position. And being less assured of his position, each man waxes increasingly more strident against Job. The tone of Job's comforters, therefore, becomes ever less coherent, even as Job himself rises to ever greater eloquence and conviction. The contrast between these two processes—Job's increasing assurance and his friends' growing insecurity—forms one of the strongest pillars in the dramatic structure of this book.

Along with the decline of moral authority among these three men, there is a corresponding decline in politeness, as though each man is obliged to raise the volume of his voice in inverse proportion to his sense of assurance. Thus, we find that Eliphaz, at least when he begins, is also the most compassionate and polite of the three comforters.

JOB 5

٭

ELIPHAZ IS SHOCKED BY JOB'S TONE. Instead of asking God to renew His mercies, Job has been cursing his own life. And since God the Creator is the author of that life, Job's lament hardly reflects well on God, says Eliphaz. This perverse attitude of Job, he reasons, must be the source of the problem. Job's affliction, consequently, is not an inexplicable mystery, as Job has argued, but the result of Job's own rebellious attitude toward God. Job's lament, Eliphaz believes, is essentially selfish, expressing only Job's subjective pain. Therefore, Eliphaz becomes more severe in his criticism of Job, referring to him as "foolish" (5:2, 3) and speaking of Job's perished children in an insensitive way (5:4).

In Eliphaz's experience of the divine claims, on which his objections to the lament of Job are based, there has been a dominant emphasis on God's utter purity and transcendence. Absolutely no created thing is pure in God's sight, neither angels (4:18) nor men (4:19). A deep humility before God, therefore, is the only attitude appropriate to man's true state.

Here Eliphaz touches a theme in the Prophets (for instance, Amos 5:4, 6), going on to describe God in terms of justice (Job 5:11–15) and benevolence (5:9, 10, 16). Eliphaz contends that Job, instead of complaining about God, even by implication, should be putting his trust in God (5:17), who delivers (5:19–20) and heals (5:18), even as He corrects and chastises.

This severity of Eliphaz will become the dominant temper of his second and third speeches (chapters 15 and 22), where he will no longer demonstrate deference and compassion toward Job. His former sympathy and concern, characteristic of chapters 4 and 5, will disappear, because Eliphaz will have repeatedly listened to Job professing his innocence. Job, Eliphaz believes, by emphatically denying a moral causality with respect to his afflictions, menaces the moral structure of the world. This is the great shortcoming of Eliphaz's comments.

What should finally be said, then, of this Edomite's argument against the suffering Job? Though it is too severe and personally insensitive,

Eliphaz does make a basically reliable case. Indeed, in God's final revelation to Job near the end of the book, we meet some of the very themes that initially appeared in the first discourse of Eliphaz.

Moreover, in the final verses of this, his first speech (5:25–26), Eliphaz ironically foretells the blessings that Job will receive at the end of the story (42:12–17). However much, then, Eliphaz managed to misinterpret the implications of his own religious experience, that experience itself was valid and sound. To say that Eliphaz was wrong in his assessment of Job does not mean that Eliphaz was wrong in respect to everything he proclaimed.

Indeed, with respect to the exchange between Eliphaz and Job, we have the impression that the two men are arguing at cross purposes. Most of Eliphaz's claims are beyond dispute, nor will Job dispute them. Above all, Job himself will bear witness to God's purity and transcendence, about which Eliphaz has been most insistent. Indeed, as the story develops we shall see that Job knows far more on this subject of God's holiness and purity than Eliphaz could imagine. The difference between the two men is that Eliphaz has never been tested as Job is being tested. Job knows this difference; Eliphaz doesn't.

JOB 6

ॐ

JOB NOW ANSWERS THE FIRST OF HIS "COMFORTERS," not with a point-by-point refutation, but by a more detailed analysis of his own experience. Each of us tends to universalize or *absolutize* his religious experience, and Job believes that this is what Eliphaz has done—he has projected his own experience onto Job. Basing his objections to Job solely on his own limited vision, Eliphaz has failed to appreciate the unique dimensions of Job's suffering.

Job says that he expected better of this friend. Eliphaz and the others know him well enough not to take him for the sinner they now imagine him to be. They have interpreted Job's sufferings as evidence of his sinful state, whereas they should be trying to see his affliction as Job himself sees it. They have not sufficiently weighed his grief, Job says (6:2).

Now Job's comments will begin to take more direct aim at God. Eliphaz, after all, has set himself up as God's spokesman, and Job's response will respect that arrangement. Eliphaz had called God "the Almighty" (*Shaddai* in 5:17), the divine title that is now taken up by Job himself (6:4, 14). That is to say, the God that Job now addresses is specifically God as identified by Eliphaz.

Job insists that his complaint is no more unreasonable than that of an animal denied its basic sustenance (6:5). He wishes that God would take away his life (6:8–10); he knows that he has not betrayed God and does not deserve this suffering.

We readers, who are familiar with the prologue of the book, are aware that Job is right. Indeed, whereas Job has only the testimony of his own conscience, we readers have the testimony of God Himself, who has already declared Job to be a just man.

Thus, when Job reproaches his friends, we readers stand with him; like dried-up streams, those friends have failed the parched traveler who looked to them with hope (6:14–20). Job has asked so little of them, nothing beyond their simple friendship (6:22–23). Instead of showing compassion for a suffering friend, however, Eliphaz has treated those sufferings of Job chiefly as an occasion to rehearse the religious convictions born of his own limited experience.

Like the friends of Job, many men are too quick to blame, especially when faced with unexplained suffering. Commenting on this chapter, St. John Chrysostom refers to the rash judgment of the citizens of Malta when they saw Paul bitten by the snake in Acts 28:4—"No doubt this man is a murderer, whom, though he has escaped the sea, yet justice does not allow to live." Similarly, the apostles, when they beheld the man born blind, immediately wanted to place the blame on somebody (John 9:2). Thus the self-appointed comforters of Job add the grievous burden of calumny to the already heavy load of his sufferings.

JOB 7

ॐ

JOB IS NO LONGER SIMPLY ANSWERING ELIPHAZ. This chapter consists, rather, of a new lament, a kind of soliloquy about the tragedies to which human existence is subject. Job likens them to three particularly miserable kinds of men: an unwilling military conscript who is in constant danger for reasons that do not interest nor concern him, a day laborer forced by his desperate circumstances to earn just enough to stay alive until he goes back to work the next day, and a slave. Human life is both hard and short, that is to say, occasionally relieved by the shadows that give a slight reprieve from the oppressive heat (7:2).

The very transitions between day and night, which in Israel's traditional wisdom literature provide a sense of stability and structure (cf. Psalms 104[103]:19–23), become in the oppressed mind of Job the source of enervating boredom, anxiety, and apathy (verses 3–4). He experiences already the corruption of death (verse 5). It is a life without hope (verses 6, 16).

Job addresses God, asking only that God will "remember" him (verse 7), for he knows that God regards him (verse 8). To die, however, as Job sees it, is to disappear even from the sight of God (verses 9–10); the finality of death is addressed several times in this book (7:21; 10:21; 14:10, 12, 18–22; 17:13–16). Death represents, for the author of Job, the major preoccupation, and a hopeful quest for a life after death is one of the deepest and most moving aspects of the book (19:25–27).

Job then begins to turn his lament into a prayer (7:11–21). His spiritual dilemma comes from the knowledge that all these terrible things have befallen him, even though throughout his life he has known God as someone who loves him and whom he loves. Has God now become his enemy? Or will God return to search for him once more? And if God does come to look for him, will He arrive too late? Will Job be already dead and gone (verses 8, 21)?

Whereas for Job's friends his sufferings raise the question of justice, for Job himself those sufferings raise, rather, a question about friendship.

Observe how, in verse 18, Job ironically alters the sense of Psalm

8:5, which asks, "What is man that You are mindful of him, and the son of man that You visit him?" Those words—"What is man?"—words that originally referred to man's grandeur, become, in the mouth of Job, a lament over man's degradation: "What is man that You should exalt him, that You set Your heart on him, that You should visit him every morning, and test him every moment?" Clearly the religious experience of Job by far transcends that of Eliphaz. Alas, his other friends will not rise even to the level of Eliphaz.

JOB 8

༄

TO THE EARS OF BILDAD, JOB'S SECOND RESPONDENT, a man even less tolerant than Eliphaz, the foregoing lament seems to be an attack on the justice of God and the entire moral order. Unlike Eliphaz, however, Bildad is able to make no argument on the basis of his own personal experience. He is obliged to argue, rather, solely from the moral tradition, which he does not understand very well. Indeed, Bildad treats the moral structure of the world in a nearly impersonal way. To the mind of Bildad, the effects of sin follow automatically, as the inevitable effects of a sufficient cause. The presence of the effect, that is, implies the presence of the cause.

If Eliphaz's argument had been too personal, bordering on the purely subjective, the argument of Bildad may be called too objective, bordering on the purely mechanical. In the mind of Bildad the principle of retributive justice functions nearly as a law of nature, or what the religions of India call the Law of Karma.

Both Eliphaz and Job show signs of knowing God personally, but we discern nothing of this in Bildad. Between Bildad and Job, therefore, there is even less of a meeting of minds than there was between Eliphaz and Job.

We should remember, on the other hand, that Job himself has never raised the abstract question of the divine justice; he has shown no interest, so far, in the problems of theodicy. Up to this point in the story, Job has been concerned only with his own problems, and his lament has been entirely personal, not theoretical.

Bildad, for his part, does not demonstrate even the limited compassion of Eliphaz. We note, for example, his comments about Job's now perished children. In the light of Job's own concern for the moral well-being of those children early in the book (1:5), there is an especially cruel irony in Bildad's speculation on their moral state: "If your sons have sinned against [God], He has cast them away for their transgression" (8:4). What a dreadful thing to say to a man who loved his sons as Job did!

Like Eliphaz before him, Bildad urges Job to repent (8:5–7), for such, he says, is the teaching of traditional morality (8:8–10).

Clearly, Bildad is unfamiliar with the God worshipped by Job, the God portrayed in the opening chapters of this book. Bildad knows nothing of a personal God who puts man to the test through the trial of his faith. Bildad's divinity is, on the contrary, a nearly mechanistic adjudicator who functions entirely as a moral arbiter of human behavior, not a loving, redemptive God who shapes man's destiny through His personal interest and intervention.

Nonetheless, in his comments about Job's final lot Bildad speaks with an unintended irony, because in fact Job's latter end *will* surpass his beginning (8:7), and "God will not cast away the *blameless*" (8:20— *tam*; cf. 1:1, 8; 2:3). On our first reading of the story, we do not know this yet, of course, because we do not know, on our first reading, how the story will end (for example 42:12).

So many comments made by Job's friends, including these by Bildad in this chapter, are full of ironic, nearly prophetic meaning, which will become clear only at the story's end, so the reader does not perceive this meaning on his first trip through the book. As Edgar Allen Poe argued in his review of *Bleak House* by Charles Dickens, the truly great stories cannot be understood on a single reading, because the entire narrative must be known before the deeper significance of the individual episodes can become manifest. As Poe remarked, we do not understand any great story well until our *second* reading of it. This insight is preeminently helpful in the case of the Book of Job.

JOB 9

჻

I<small>F WE FIND</small> J<small>OB BECOMING INCREASINGLY DESPONDENT</small> through the course of this book, let us bear in mind that he is responding to friends who prove themselves increasingly obtuse and insensitive. Bildad, in his objections to Job, was far worse than Eliphaz. Job's response to Bildad follows the same threefold outline that we saw in his response to Eliphaz in chapters 6—7. There is a direct response (9:2–24), a soliloquy (9:25—10:1), and an address to God (10:1–22).

Ironically, in Job's direct response, which takes up most of this chapter, he largely ignores the self-righteous ranting of Bildad. Indeed, we have the impression that Job has "tuned out" Bildad at some point and gone on to recall Eliphaz's earlier comment (4:17) about man's inability to be just in the sight of God.

That earlier remark of Eliphaz posed for Job a problem he addresses in the present chapter. If God's will is that which determines justice, and there is no other measure of justice to be consulted, how does a man of clean conscience deal with the problem of suffering? (This is, of course, the great problem of theodicy. Job's analysis of it, however, is not theoretical; he has too much personal pain for purely abstract thought.) If man is unable to perceive God as acting justly, must he not think of God as acting in anger? And how can man perceive God's anger as just, in the absence of any condign self-accusation in his own conscience? Job knows that God is near, but he cannot discern the path that God is following (9:11).

Job's impulse is not to answer God in this respect, but rather to supplicate Him (9:15). Is there no difference between God's violent treatment of nature (9:4–5) and His violent treatment of man (9:17–18)? Is God's justice truly indistinguishable from His power (9:19)? Is justice rational, or merely willful?

Meanwhile, even as he ponders these deep, perplexing questions, Job seems to be dying (9:25–26), and he fears dying without being reconciled to God (9:30–33). Truly his plight is dire.

JOB 10

ॐ

JOB REASONS THAT GOD MUST BE DIFFERENT from what his friends believe Him to be. If these friends have so wrongly judged Job, whom they do see, how can they rightly judge God, whom they do not see?

Job essays in this chapter, then, various theories to elucidate the problem under consideration, only to reject all those theories in the end. Is God cruel (verse 3), or deceived (verse 4), or shortsighted (verse 5) with respect to Job? No, Job answers. God knows that he is innocent (verse 7).

Having mentioned God's "hand" in verse 7 ("*there is* no one who can deliver from Your hand"), Job goes on, in verses 8–12, to meditate on God's fashioning him by hand ("Your hands have made me and fashioned me"). This moving text is especially reminiscent of Psalm 139(138):13–15.

All this care did God take in this creation and preservation; was everything for naught, Job wonders? Does he himself value this "life and mercy," Job inquires, more than God does? Not a bit. God holds these matters in His heart, he says (verse 13). Feeling full of confusion at such thoughts, Job pleads only that God look upon his sufferings (verse 15).

Aware that he is not a wicked man, Job is compelled to imagine that God afflicts the just as well as the unjust, for reasons best known to Himself (verses 16–17). We readers, in fact, know this to be the case. We know exactly what those reasons are. We have the advantage of overhearing those early conversations between God and Satan in the first two chapters of the book.

In this respect we readers of the Book of Job enjoy a great interpretive edge over the human characters within the story itself, because from the very beginning of the story we have known its true dynamics and direction. Remembering that Job is being tried by a God who has great confidence in him, we readers are entirely on Job's side in this contest and hope he will not fail his period of probation. For this reason we also know that the speculations of Job's three friends are far wide of the mark.

At the same time, especially as Job expresses his longings in these lengthy soliloquies, we readers become conscious of the deeper dimensions of his character, levels of soul more profound than what might have been expected of that observant doer of God's will introduced back in chapter 1. God, of course, has known these things all along; God was already thoroughly familiar with Job's heart.

Throughout the story we ourselves are gradually given an insight into that heart, perceiving dimensions that we might not have anticipated. We begin to discern Job's radical longing for God, his deep need for God's approval. Though the verb itself is not used in the text, we are looking at a man that actually *loves* God.

JOB 11

⟿

WE NOW COME TO THE FIRST SPEECH OF ZOPHAR, Job's most strident critic, a man who can appeal to neither personal religious experience (as did Eliphaz) nor inherited moral tradition (as did Bildad). Possessed of neither resource, Zophar's contribution is what we may call "third-hand." He bases his criticism on his own theory of wisdom. Although he treats his theory as self-evidently true, we recognize it as only a personal bias.

Moreover, Zophar seems to identify his own personal perception of wisdom as the wisdom of God Himself. Whereas Bildad had endeavored to defend the divine justice, Zophar tries to glorify "divine" wisdom in Job's case. If it is difficult to see justice verified in Job's sufferings, however, it is even harder to see wisdom verified by those sufferings.

Like the two earlier speakers, Zophar calls on Job to repent in order to regain the divine favor. (This is a rather common misunderstanding that claims, "If things aren't going well for you, you should go figure out how you have offended God, because He is obviously displeased with you.")

Zophar also resorts to sarcasm. Although this particular rhetorical form is perfectly legitimate in some circumstances (and the prophets, beginning with Elijah, use it often), sarcasm becomes merely an instrument of cruelty when directed at someone who is suffering incomprehensible pain. In the present case, Job suffers in an extreme way, pushed to the very limits of his endurance. It is such a one that Zophar has the vile temerity to call a "man full of talk" (11:2), a liar (11:3), a vain man (11:11–12), and wicked (11:14, 20).

The final two verses (19–20) contain an implied warning against the "death wish" to which Job has several times given voice. This very sentiment, Zophar says, stands as evidence of Job's wickedness.

The author of the Book of Job surely understands this extended criticism by Zophar as an exercise in irony. Though the context of his speech proves the speaker himself insensitive and nearly irrational in his personal cruelty, there is an undeniable eloquence in his description of the divine wisdom (11:7–9) and his assertion of the moral quality of human existence (11:10–12). Moreover, those very rewards that Zophar promises to Job in the event of his repentance (11:13–18) do, in fact, fall into Job's life at the end of the book.

In this story of Job, men are not divided into those who have wisdom and those who don't. In the Book of Job *no one* is really wise. There is no real wise man, as there is in, say, the Book of Proverbs. While wisdom is ever present in the plot of the story, no character in the story has a clear grasp of it. True wisdom will not stand manifest until God, near the end of the narrative, speaks for Himself. Even then God will not disclose to Job the particulars of His dealings with him throughout the story.

JOB 12

༈

JOB NOW BEGINS A SPEECH (12:1—14:22) that is his longest until the final soliloquy in the book. Having just received a blast of sarcasm from Zophar, and now aware that all three of his friends are against him, Job himself takes up the weapon of sarcasm, and to considerable effect. He already knew, after all, everything that his friends have been telling him. Indeed, much of it was of the commonest knowledge. Though he had looked to his friends for insight, they have hitherto provided only truisms and platitudes.

Unlike his three friends, Job knows there is a mystery involved in his sufferings, and he endeavors to identify it. Tell me something new, he says to them, not things we all know already and are already agreed upon. Anyone with eyes in his head, Job argues, can see that the wicked sometimes really do prosper (verse 6). This much is not news. Might it not also be the case, however, that the just sometimes really do suffer?

Of course, God governs the world and all things, including the destinies of men (verse 10), but if the prosperity of the wicked is compatible with the governance of God, might not the suffering of the just also be consonant with the governance of God? Who among men has so clear an understanding of God that God can be reduced simply to a component in some human theory of justice?

These matters are not to be rashly concluded, says Job. They should, rather, be tested and probed, much as the ear of a writer tries various words, and the mouth of the cook tests various recipes (verse 11).

Indeed, the entire Book of Job, exploring the mystery of God's justice and providence, is an example and illustration of such testing. Those who would speak for God, especially if they speak to a man who is suffering, should not pretend that they really see things as God does. This has been the offense of Job's friends. They imagine themselves to be speaking for the Almighty, but in fact they are only trying words and testing recipes. Nothing more.

God will overthrow their theories (verse 20), bringing deep things out of darkness (verse 22). Left to their own lights, men grope about in this darkness (verses 24–25). In this respect, Job's friends are no wiser than he.

The difference between the two cases is not a matter of wisdom, therefore, any more than it is a matter of justice. The difference between Job and his friends is that Job is suffering, while they are "at ease" (verse 5). They have been using this advantage solely to pass judgment on a suffering human being, who differs from them only by the fact that he is suffering. This is a great moral offense.

JOB 13

Has Eliphaz experienced God (4:8; 5:3, 27)? Well, so has Job (13:1–2). Indeed, throughout these discussions Job is the only person who has actually *addressed* God. Job's three friends have set themselves to speak *for* God, but it is significant that not one of them has yet spoken *to* God. Job, in contrast, has never tried to speak *for* God. It is God Himself that Job would address (13:3). He wants to "reason *with*" God, not reason *about* God.

And all the reasoning about God with which his friends have been occupied, says Job, is a pack of lies (13:4). Unable to perceive that the ways of God are mysterious and inscrutable, they have succeeded only in elaborating a moral theory that discredits the Almighty by denying the subtlety of the divine wisdom. They themselves would display more wisdom if they simply kept quiet (13:5). Such a silence would at least keep them from speaking "wickedly for God" (13:7).

Verses 6–11 begin with the plural form of the Deuteronomic "Hear!" (also in verse 17) and go on to ask a series of questions, each line of which begins with the Hebrew interrogative prefix *ha* (the Hebrew equivalent of the question mark in English). Job thus beats back his critics with a chain of unanswerable questions.

In verse 14 Job begins his "reasoning with" God, an exercise that consists in the "pleadings" of his lips (cf. verse 6). These pleadings are a combination of questions and prayers in which Job's deepest soul and most anguished longings are laid bare before the Almighty. His trust in God will never be destroyed, he declares (verse 16), for God is his "salvation" (*Yoshuah* = Jesus).

Job is urgently concerned for his standing in God's eyes. Indeed, this is his sole concern. He wants nothing more than to be pleasing to God. Unlike his friends, Job knows, in an absolute sort of way, that more is happening in his life than meets the eye. If this were not the case, Job is sure, his sufferings would be senseless.

If these sufferings cannot be interpreted as a divine punishment, then what do they mean? In addressing this query, Job is feeling his way tentatively toward what we have called the Bible's apocalyptic principle, according to which "more is happening than seems to be happening." In the "pleadings" of this chapter, Job's mind is faced with a blank wall with no cracks through which he might see the reality just on the other side of his pain. This pain of his yearning, questioning heart is far sharper than the afflictions in his flesh.

JOB 14

THIS CHAPTER HAS A DIALECTICAL STRUCTURE. Starting from an individual lament, in which Job attends to his personal pain and the longings of his own heart, he turns to a general reflection about what is today called "the *human* situation" (as distinct from "*my* situation"). He reflects on the short and troubled life of "man" (*adam*) born of a "woman" (*ishsha*). The very measuring of man's time on earth, the determined numbering of his allotted days, becomes for Job the symbol and reminder of the larger and more encompassing limitations that mark human existence (verse 5).

A tree, in fact, is harder to kill than a man, because of the depth of its root. The unfeeling tree, which has never reflected on its existence at all, may yet find the resources to go on living, even though it is cut off at ground level: "There is hope for a tree" (*yesh la'ets*). The tree thrives by reason of its burial in the earth. Man, in contrast, once he is buried in the earth, simply disappears. At least if "man" is considered abstractly—that is to say, regarded from outside—this seems to be the case (verses 6–12).

At this point, however, Job stops regarding man from outside and begins once again to inspect the impulses of his own heart, touching on an underlying preoccupation of his mind. Specifically, he begins to consider his own natural aspiration for an afterlife and his innate suspicion, spawned of a prior hope (which seems native to the structure of his heart), that God will not disappoint that suspicion: "Oh, that You would hide me in the grave, . . . You shall call, and I will answer You" (verses 13, 15). Even as he lies in his grave, Job will await the summoning voice of God. Will God remember him? Will he hear that voice, "Lazarus, come forth"? With all his heart, Job longs for that day and the vindication of that hope.

The Christian, who reads Holy Scripture as a single body of canonical literature, will recognize Job's hope as the prelude to a higher promise: "Do not marvel at this; for the hour is coming in which all who are in the graves will hear His voice and come forth" (John 5:28–29).

At this point, however, Job himself can hear only a quieter voice whispering faintly in his heart. His is the faith of Enoch, who believed that God exists "and *that* He is a rewarder of those who diligently seek Him" (Hebrews 11:6).

This hope of Job's heart is organic to his experience and inseparable from the deeper impulses of his soul. It is not, like the hope of Socrates in the *Phaedo*, a theoretical hope. It is spawned of a spiritual instinct, not of critical reflection. Consequently, when Job starts once again (in verse 18) to reflect on the question abstractly and to argue the point dialectically, he cannot justify this hope to his critical mind. Born solely from a faint and innate perception, this hope cannot yet survive critical dissection, so the end of the chapter finds Job falling yet once more into despondency.

Indeed, at this point Job seems to lose even the modest, meager expectation of the worldly man: namely, that he may live on in his children (verse 21). In any case, alas, Job no longer has any children. From a worldly perspective, Job's existence is a total wreck.

Behold the dilemma of Job's mind. If he consults solely the personal impulses of his soul, Job knows that he loves God and strongly suspects that God loves him. When, however, he begins to regard human existence in the detached abstraction of critical thought, death appears as the very end, and all man's hope is doomed (verse 19). One suspects that Job, if he had died at this point in the story, would have finished his life begging, like Goethe, "More Light!"

JOB 15

ॐ

WITH THIS CHAPTER WE START THE SECOND CYCLE of speeches. Once again, Eliphaz speaks first. (He seems to be the eldest; cf. verse 10).

In his former discourse (chapters 4—5) Eliphaz showed respect and even a measure of sympathy for the suffering Job, treating him as a basically righteous man who had somehow incurred the divine wrath by some unknown offense. He exhorted Job, then, to examine his conscience more carefully, to discern what that hidden offense against God might be, and to repent of it.

That simple attitude of sympathy and concern for Job, however, is no longer possible; Eliphaz has listened to Job repeatedly profess his innocence of any such offense. Since that first speech of Eliphaz, Job has altered the very suppositions of their discourse by separating his sufferings from any simple concepts of either justice or wisdom.

It now seems to Eliphaz that Job, by emphatically denying a causal relationship between his sins and his afflictions, menaces the moral structure of the world itself, and Eliphaz responds with both aggression and, in the closing verses of the chapter, even a tone of threat.

Is Job older than Adam, he asks, or as old as wisdom itself (verse 7; cf. Proverbs 8:25), that he should be engaged in such dangerous speculations about the hidden purposes of God?

The irony here, of course, is that Job is the only one whose discourse manifests even a shred of intellectual humility. Job has never, like Eliphaz (4:12–21), claimed to discern the divine mind.

Yet it is true that Job, driven by his distress, has probed the matter of suffering more deeply. Job has sensed that something mysterious is at play in the sad fortunes of his recent life, something hinted at in Eliphaz's own expression, "the [secret] counsel of God" (verse 8). Job himself will later use this identical expression, *sod Eloah*, to describe his friendship with God in the earlier part of his life (29:4).

In the first two chapters of this book, we readers were given a glimpse into that secret counsel of God. God's "secret counsel" is the essence of His mysterious intervention in human history (Ephesians

49

3:9), including the individual lives of His loyal servants (Romans 8:28).

Job's sustained probing after that secret counsel is what offends Eliphaz, the older man who considers such probing investigation a symptom of arrogance (verses 9, 12–13). There is nothing "hidden" going on, Eliphaz declares (verse 18); the moral structure of human existence, including the principle of inevitable retribution, has long been plain to human understanding (verses 20–35). Thus, the suffering Job is getting only what he deserves.

JOB 16

⁂

JOB MUST NOW ANSWER THE SCATHING INDICTMENT that he has just received from Eliphaz. His response, which generally takes the form of lament and complaint, contains some of the most memorable and moving verses of the book, chiefly his appeal to the heavenly Witness of his sufferings.

Just exchange souls (*nephesh*, as in Genesis 2:8) with me, Job tells his companions (the "you" here being plural), and you will understand (verse 4). I certainly would not treat you as you are treating me (verse 5). If their roles were reversed, says Job, he would be a worthier comforter. He would not add to their suffering but would assuage their grief.

Job finds that neither speech nor silence can avail (verse 6). He kept silence, but it provided him no wisdom. He spoke with his companions, seeking help to understand, but this brought him only further ignomiy. In both cases his sufferings continued.

At this point, however, Job stops speaking to his companions and once again addresses God. (The reader observes that Job is always at his best when he speaks to God.) Eliphaz, he complains, has attacked him with the fury of a wild beast (verse 9), and so have the others. Indeed, God Himself has handed Job over to their reproaches (verse 11), and they inexplicably afflict him with every manner of suffering (verses 12–17). (This text is one of those that best indicate why the Eastern Orthodox Church reads the Book of Job during Holy Week.)

But suddenly, in the midst of this lament, Job appeals to God to bear witness to this terrible taking of his innocent life. Using terms reminiscent of the unjustly slain Abel, he tells the earth not to cover the innocent blood that cries to heaven with "pure prayer" (verses 17–18; cf. Genesis 4:10; Isaiah 26:21; Ezekiel 24:8; Hebrews 12:24).

And who in heaven will hear Job's cry? The Witness, the very God in whom Job has ever placed his trust (verse 19). Let men on earth say what they will; Job sends his appeal on high. As the chapter ends, Job seems resolved to die without understanding what terrible thing has transpired to make him die in such misery of soul and body. But God is his Witness; God will see, and Job leaves his case to God.

No matter how vehement his frequent complaints, Job always returns to this conviction that "God sees and knows." All his life long, Job has endeavored to live in the sight of God. God has always been his Witness, the One who reads his heart. This cultivated awareness, at the root of Job's character, is the source of his strength to endure.

JOB 17

_ॐ_

It is the teaching of all of Holy Scripture that our mortality is the Fall that we sinners inherit from Adam. In other words, "through one man sin entered the world, and death through sin" (Romans 5:12). We have it on this same authority that "by the one man's offense death reigned through the one" (5:17). In short, "sin reigned in death" (5:21).

It is the teaching of the Christian Church that by reason of Adam's Fall, man without Christ is under the reign of death and corruption, because "the reign of death operates only in the corruption of the flesh" (Tertullian, _On the Resurrection_ 47).

As the physical expression of sin, death chiefly represents man's final and definitive separation from God. That is to say, apart from Christ, death is simply sin in its final stage. It embodies everything that sin means. It is the ultimate alienation from God. Consequently, if there is one sure general characteristic of death in the Old Testament, it is death's utter separation of a man from the knowledge, remembrance, and praise of God.

Thus, King Hezekiah, after his own very close encounter with the grave, commented that what he most feared about death was its concomitant exclusion from the praise of God: "For Sheol cannot thank You, / Death cannot praise You; / Those who go down to the pit cannot hope for Your truth" (Isaiah 38:18). "For in death _there is_ no remembrance of You," lamented David; "In the grave who will give You thanks?" (Psalm 6:5). And the sons of Korah mourned, "Shall Your lovingkindness be declared in the grave? / _Or_ Your faithfulness in the place of destruction? / Shall Your wonders be known in the dark? / And Your righteousness in the land of forgetfulness?" (Psalm 88[87]:11–12).

Always there is that same rhetorical question: "Who shall praise the Most High in the grave?" (Sirach 17:27)—"What profit _is there_ in my blood, / When I go down to the pit? / Will the dust praise You? / Will it declare Your truth?" (Psalm 30[29]:9). It was the common doctrine of the Old Testament that "the dead who are in the graves, whose souls are taken from their bodies, will give unto the Lord neither praise nor righteousness" (Baruch 2:17). It is in the Book of Job, as we shall see in due course, that this perspective of death's finality is most forcefully challenged in the Old Testament.

Still, the notion of an "afterlife with God," following death, is entirely alien to the Hebrew Scriptures. Indeed, it is also alien to the New Testament, unless a person has died in the redemptive faith of Christ. It is Christ alone who delivers man from death, including the saints of the Old Testament. Nowhere in the Bible is there an after*life* apart from Christ. Whatever after*existence* there may be apart from Christ, it is certainly no real *life*.

This hopeless Old Testament view of death, then, is what Job is facing in the present chapter. He is staring at death's approach, his entrance into "the land of forgetfulness," his final separation from the One whom he has loved and trusted all his life, and he is doing so with no sense of God's presence or His favor. The dark words of this chapter, nonetheless, will not be Job's last comment on the subject of death and corruption.

JOB 18

❧

Bɪʟᴅᴀᴅ ᴄᴏɴᴛᴇɴᴅs ᴛʜᴀᴛ ʜᴇ ᴀɴᴅ ʜɪs ᴛᴡᴏ ᴄᴏᴍᴘᴀɴɪᴏɴs have been sharing with Job the rock-solid truth on which the moral life is founded. Job, however, has insisted on moving this rock (18:4). Does Job believe that the eternal principles of the moral order should be adjusted to suit his own case?

Bildad goes on to elaborate the punishments that wicked men, such as Job, must expect (18:5–11). His references to darkness (18:5–6, 18) appear especially severe when we bear in mind how desperately Job has sought enlightenment in his plight.

Bildad's second speech is particularly cruel in its judgment of Job, listing each of his afflictions in turn as evidence of his guilt. For example, Job has just spoken of the approaching darkness of the grave (17:12–14). Now Bildad takes up that very theme against him (18:5–6, 18). Job has just mentioned his failing strength (17:7, 18), and Bildad turns it into sarcastic obloquy (18:7, 12–13). Job lamented that onlookers were shocked at his condition (17:6, 8), and Bildad makes the point a matter of further reproach (18:20). The grave that Job described as his future home (17:13–16) is evidence to Bildad that he is "a man who does not know God" (18:21). In short, Job shows every symptom of a man whom God has rightly abandoned, and Bildad makes even his sufferings a reproach to him.

Bildad, in this second speech, thus abandons even the scant sympathy expressed in his first. He further rehearses, rather, his simplistic and illogical claim that all human suffering can be reduced to the inevitable consequence of the sins of the man who suffers. This impersonal, even mechanical theory of moral retribution more closely resembles the Hindu "law of karma" and the Buddhist "chain of causation" than it does anything taught in Holy Scripture.

Moreover, in its emphatic denial of this mechanical and impersonal theory of sin and retribution, the teaching of the Book of Job on the mystery (*sod*) of human suffering, especially the suffering of the innocent and the just, prepares the believing mind for the more ample doctrine of the Cross, whereon an innocent and just Man suffered and died for the sake of the guilty and the unjust. The trial of Job was preparatory to the trial of Jesus. It is ultimately the Cross that vindicates Job's cause.

This vindication by the Cross especially pertains to Job's preoccupation with death and corruption. The Just Man who died on the Cross, tormented by the bystanders as a person rejected by God (Matthew 27:39–43), is identical with the Holy One who was not suffered to see corruption (Acts 2:27).

JOB 19

❦

THIS IS ARGUABLY THE FINEST CHAPTER in the Book of Job, containing his most memorable profession of faith.

Up to this point in the book, Job has attempted various "soundings" of the mystery of his sufferings, and these themes are remembered again in the present chapter. Thus, he speaks once again of the testimony of his conscience (6:30; 9:29; 10:7; 16:17), his appeal to God's justice (10:2, 7; 13:23; 16:21), his sense of God's friendship (7:8, 21; 10:8–9; 14:15), his desire for God's vindication of his case (14:13–15; 16:19–20). This last theme, Job's desire for God's vindication, dominates the closing section of the chapter.

Job begins by wondering why his friends feel so threatened by his reaction to his predicament (19:4). Are they really so unsure of themselves and their theories? What, after all, do they have to lose? Job is dealing with God (19:6), not them, and the problem is on God's side, not Job's (19:7). Job argues that his sufferings do not come from some inexorable law (19:8–12), as Bildad supposes (cf. 18:5–10), but from God's intentional choice.

Indeed, it was God who sent these alleged comforters to make him even more miserable (19:12–15, 19), to say nothing of his wife (verse 17)! He is wasting away (19:20) and now pleads for pity from these professed friends (19:21–22).

Then come the truly shining lines of the book, where Job places all his hope in God, his "Redeemer" or Vindicator in the latter days (verses 23–27). This noun, go'el, is the active participial form of the verb ga'al, meaning "to avenge."

Both the noun and the verb are often used in the Hebrew Bible with reference to God Himself, and in these instances the Christian transmission of Holy Scripture has preferred the words "redeem" and "purchase" to translate this Hebrew verb. Thus, Psalm 74(73):2 says that God "redeemed" or "purchased" (ga'alta) His people in their Exodus from Egypt. Similarly, God is called the "Redeemer" (Go'el) of the fatherless (Proverbs 23:11; cf. Jeremiah 50:34). Such expressions are very common in the Book of Psalms (for example, 69:19 [68:18]; 107 [106]:2).

Particularly to the point with reference to the Book of Job is the use of this verb, *ga'al*, when it means deliverance from death or the underworld (Sheol). This context is found in Psalm 103(102):4 and Hosea 13:14.

When Job calls God his *Go'el*, therefore, he is speaking with the common voice of Holy Scripture. The Lord is explicitly invoked by this name in Psalm 19:15 (18:14) and 78(77):35. In the second part of the Book of Isaiah this word is a standard epithet for God (41:14; 43:14; 44:6; 47:4; 48:17; 49:7, 8, 26; 54:5; 60:16; 63:16).

Job's *Go'el* is identical to his heavenly Witness *('edh)* in 16:19–20 and his "Spokesman" *(melits)* in 9:33 and 33:23.

Job's appeal here is entirely eschatological. That is to say, he lays all his hope in God's final, future, definitive judgment.

Until that day, and in testimony to that hope, Job wants these words inscribed in stone. Here we have the Hebrew Scriptures' clearest expression of hope for the resurrection of the dead and the final vision of God. This chapter is one of direct preparation for the New Testament and the glory of the Resurrection.

JOB 20

୬ଚ

THROUGH THE VARIOUS SOLILOQUIES, prayers, and discourses of Job, we may observe a distinct development and maturing of his thought. The critical observations of his friends, even their insults and obloquy, force him to examine his own ideas and perceptions more critically, to try fresh paths of reflection, to probe his problem anew from previously untried perspectives. Job's mind is not monochrome; it actually changes and grows richer throughout the course of the book.

With Job's three friends, the very opposite is true. In the eight responses that they make to him, the reader observes that the thought-content, if it can be said to alter at all, rather grandly declines. Job grows, that is to say, while his friends diminish.

The first speaker was Eliphaz, who largely based his argument against Job on his personal experience, his religious vision, insight, or *veda*. Although the thought of Eliphaz is certainly *found wanting* in the full context of the Book of Job, his first discourse did represent, in fact, a solid nucleus of profound insight. Eliphaz was, so to speak, an eyewitness. He represented a living contact with genuine religious experience. Whole civilizations could be constructed on the teachings of Eliphaz.

Next came Bildad, however, whose argument against Job appealed, not to any religious or metaphysical experience of his own, but to the inherited and established teaching of his elders. Bildad represents, as it were, the *next* generation of thinkers, and in the transition from Eliphaz to Bildad we observed insight declining into theory. Bildad was no eyewitness, but more of a character witness. He represented a tradition rather than an insight. Bildad's ideas, compared with those of Eliphaz, were not vibrant. Indeed, they were somewhat stale.

Finally, when we came to Zophar's contribution, there was neither insight nor theory, but mere opinion and prejudice. Moving through the arguments of these three men, we perceived a decline of insight into tradition, and tradition into bias. The respective arguments of Job's friends, that is to say, followed a downward path.

Now, as these same three speakers take their second turns to speak, their arguments have become even worse, because each man can do no more than repeat what he said before, only this time in a much louder and more strident voice: "What?! Didn't you hear me the first time?!"

The loudest and harshest of these is Zophar, who had neither insight nor theory even to start with. Zophar never possessed any argument stronger than a prejudice, and his second attempt is simply a more obstreperous version of the first.

Zophar's speech here in chapter 20 and Bildad's in chapter 18 serve as two sides to frame Job's great profession of faith in chapter 19. The contrast between Job's inspiring, living profession and the moldy, repeated vituperations of these two men could not be starker. The present chapter is Zophar's perverted fantasy about what an evil man Job must be and what a terrible divine judgment awaits him. It sounds all the more ridiculous and improbable because it so closely follows on the grandeur of Job's aspirations in the previous chapter.

JOB 21

૭૭

MOST OF THIS CHAPTER IS JOB'S EXAMINATION of the considerable empirical evidence that stands against the thesis of his friends. Job only argues here; he does not pray. Psychologically strengthened by his own affirmation of faith two chapters earlier, he now goes on the offensive against these mean, narrow men who have made themselves his critics. They have contended all along that God blesses the virtuous and punishes the wicked, and that this principle of retributive justice is manifest in Job's own fate. Oh, says Job, is this so clear?

The example elicited by Job is not the obvious villain, the wicked tyrant proposed by Eliphaz (15:20) and Zophar (20:12–14, 18), because such a person cannot truly be called happy. Job proposes, rather, the simply godless man, who has no time for God nor sees why he should. Such a one is sufficiently happy with his lot in this world, so why bother about God? Does not this example indicate that goodness and good fortune are not necessarily inseparable things?

Indeed, it seems to be the case that prosperity itself may actually prompt a man to adopt godless sentiments (verses 14–15). Still, says Job, we see irreligious men enjoying God's benefits, rather much as his three friends claim is the lot solely of God-fearing men.

Take the blessings that Eliphaz predicates of the religious man in 5:20–26. These blessings also fall to the lot of the irreligious man described by Job here in verses 8–13. Such a one receives God's precious gifts, such as children (verse 8), homes (verse 9), possessions (verse 10), and happiness (verse 11). Truth to tell, are not these the blessings that Job himself formerly knew? But an ungodly, irreligious man may have these things as well.

And then that same may also die a painless death (verse 13). Moreover, does not death itself suggest that God is something less than discriminating in the outpouring of His benedictions? Death befalls everyone, just and unjust alike (verses 23–26). Just where, then, is all this justice that established the world?

Dr. S. M. Hutchens has summarized very well the metaphysical problem uncovered in this chapter of Job: "I believe that one of the fundamental insights of the Book of Job is that theodicy is *always* a losing game. God cannot be justified, by Reason, reasons, or reasoning. The only argument for God is God Himself. . . . No matter how much a man has suffered or received in his suffering, it does not qualify him to serve as God's attorney."

JOB 22

In this, his third speech, Eliphaz the Temanite abandons all restraint in his response to Job. Did not Job's most recent comments, after all, completely overthrow the moral order? No more, then, will Eliphaz demonstrate the forbearance that somewhat characterized his first speech (chapters 4—5), nor even the (Eliphaz would say) restrained tone of his second (chapter 15). He now regards Job as the utter skeptic and unbeliever that his most recent remarks prove him to be.

We observe how Eliphaz, having started from the highest moral authority among the three comforters, sinks now to the lowest. This moral decline demonstrates the Latin adage, *corruptio optimi pessima*, or, as Shakespeare rephrased it, "Lilies that fester smell far worse than weeds." We know that Eliphaz is a religious man, but now his religion is put at the service of intellectual and moral distortion, as he accuses Job of the vilest crimes, especially cruelty to the poor (verses 6–9).

No point of this accusation against Job, of course, can be sustained by evidence. Eliphaz *never* appeals to evidence, however. His arguments are entirely *a priori*, arguments "from principle." He has no empirical evidence for Job's sins. These alleged offenses of Job are but inferences drawn from Eliphaz's theory. Unfortunately his theory is wrong.

The error displayed in the argument of Eliphaz is the one that logicians call the *AC fallacy*, "affirming the consequent." It is the kind of argument that asserts that, because athletes must be strong, all strong people must be athletes.

This very common formal logical fallacy consists in the misguided attempt to argue from an inference (or consequent) to a premise (or antecedent); that is to say, it is the attempt to reverse the terms of a hypothesis.

This description may sound complicated, but another example renders it easier to understand.

Let us look at the following hypothetical syllogism, which is perfectly valid: "(A) If I steal all the money in Chase Manhattan Bank, I will be wealthy. (B) I have stolen all the money in Chase Manhattan

Bank. (C) Therefore, I am wealthy." The juxtaposition of these two antecedents or premises (A and B) leads logically to the consequent or inference (C). This is a sound exercise in logic.

The *AC fallacy*, however, which "affirms the consequent," endeavors to reverse the process of that valid hypothetical syllogism. It turns the argument backwards by simply "affirming the consequent" of the hypothesis. Sticking with the same example, the *AC fallacy* says: "(A) If I steal all the money in Chase Manhattan Bank, I will be wealthy. (B) I am wealthy. (C) Therefore, I must have stolen all the money in Chase Manhattan Bank!"

We immediately sense that something is wrong with this argument, because it implies that wealthy people are necessarily thieves. This argument is fallacious on its face, because we know that there are all sorts of ways of becoming wealthy besides recourse to bank robbery.

This kind of fallacy, though somewhat common, is easily spotted by inspection, as the present example shows, and we would expect a man of Eliphaz's intellectual culture to detect it readily.

Instead, Eliphaz has been using that same fallacy to argue against Job. He is saying, "(A) People suffer for it if they sin. (B) Job is suffering. (C) Therefore, Job must have sinned." Just as there are all sorts of explanations for wealth besides bank robbery, however, so there are all sorts of explanations for personal suffering besides personal sin.

The narrow moral imagination of Eliphaz, nonetheless, is incapable of considering such possibilities. He has had a personal religious experience that he described earlier in the book, and he bases his entire moral theory on the limited insight derived from that experience. He had a vision one night, and his hair stood on end (4:15), and now he thinks he "knows it all." In this he presumes to be God's spokesman (verses 21–30).

JOB 23

❦

HAVING LISTENED TO ELIPHAZ'S THIRD DISCOURSE, Job apparently feels, "Why bother?" Consequently, in this chapter he limits his rebuttal of Eliphaz to a brief and entirely oblique repudiation of the latter's slanders against him (verses 11–12).

As Job was entirely argumentative in chapter 21, so in these next two chapters he becomes entirely meditative. The tone of these two chapters is deeply sad, notwithstanding Job's high assertion of faith in chapter 19. His mood is more somber now, as he reflects on God's inaccessibility. If chapter 18 represented Job's pillar of fire, the present discourse is his pillar of cloud, and both experiences are integral to his testing. Now he longs for a God that he cannot reach: "Oh, that I knew where I might find Him" (verse 3).

In verses 8–10 Job describes his sense of God's absence in terms reminiscent of the psalmist's description of God's presence (cf. Psalm 139[138]). A comparison of these two texts is instructive. The Psalmist found God in whatever direction he turned: "You have hedged me behind and before, / And laid Your hand upon me" (Psalm 139:5). God, that is to say, is in front and in back of him. God is also on either side of him: "Even there Your hand shall lead me, / And Your right hand hold me" (139:10). In short, the Psalmist finds that he can go nowhere and escape the presence of God: "Where can I go from Your Spirit? / Or where can I flee from Your presence?" (139:7).

Like the Psalmist, Job seeks God in every direction: "I go forward, but He is not *there*, / And backward, but I cannot perceive Him; / When He works on the left hand, I cannot behold *Him*; / When He turns to the right hand, I cannot see *Him*" (verses 8–9). In short, Job's experience seems, at first, to be the opposite of that in Psalm 139. Whereas the Psalmist found God everywhere, Job finds Him nowhere. As Eric Voegelin observed when commenting on this text of Job, "the search in space no longer reveals a divine presence" (*Israel and Revelation* [Volume 14 of *Order and History*], page 76).

It must be said, nonetheless, that this contrast between Job and the

Psalmist is more apparent than real. Job is no skeptic about the divine presence. Indeed, he is overpowered by it: "Therefore I am terrified at His presence; / When I consider *this*, I am afraid of Him. / For God made my heart weak, / And the Almighty terrifies me" (verses 15–16).

In each case, moreover, there is the profound sense of *being known* by God. Thus, the Psalmist began his meditation, "O LORD, You have searched me and known *me* (*vatteda'*) . . . . You comprehend my path . . . And are acquainted with all my ways (*derakai*)" (Psalm 139:1, 3). Job, for his part, affirms no less: "But He knows the way (*yada' derek*) that I take; / *When* He has tested me, I shall come forth as gold" (verse 10).

The Psalmist does, in fact, finish his meditation with sentiments that we easily associate with the soul of Job: "Search me, O God, and know my heart; / Try me, and know my anxieties; / And see if *there is any* wicked way in me, / And lead me in the way everlasting" (Psalm 139:23–24).

JOB 24

❧

THE PRESENT CHAPTER CONTINUES JOB'S SEVENTH RESPONSE to his critics. Here he leaves the limiting confines of his own experience to reflect more generally on man's miserable estate. This reflection continues the startling challenge that Job had made in chapter 21, offering further evidence to dispute the "moral universe" idea defended by his three friends.

To these men, who have been consistently asserting that those who suffer deserve to suffer, Job raises the spectacle of those who clearly suffer unjustly. God sees all such suffering (verse 1), but He does not intervene, says Job.

Thus, men are obliged to endure the theft of their property (verses 2–4). They must bear with homelessness and exposure (verses 7–8). They have to sustain injustice and oppression (verses 9, 12). Hunger presses upon them (verse 10). Those thus oppressed do not deserve such things. But does God put a stop to all these moral outrages (verse 12)? Manifestly He does not.

Thus Job demolishes the theory that suffering is solely the lot of the wicked. Those who would defend the justice of God must do so in a way that takes seriously these sad facts of life.

And if the evidence shows that the just must sometimes endure injustice, is it not also true that the unjust go unpunished? Is it so obvious that God invariably chastises the sinner? Does God, for instance, invariably bring retribution on the murderer (verse 14)? Is it always the case that the adulterer is reproved (verse 15)? Does it never happen that the thief goes unpunished (verse 16)? Those who glibly contend that the world is founded on divine justice, says Job, had better take a closer look at such evidence!

Job is not arguing that God is unjust, of course, nor is he denying that justice itself is rooted in the structure of created existence. He is simply asserting that the evidence is complex and not easy to grasp. Job is taking seriously the classical problem of theodicy: How do we reconcile the existence of an all-wise, all-just, and all-knowing God with the simultaneous existence of evil?

Against his own accusers, Job is arguing that goodness and good fortune are not invariably and in every instance entwined. The simplest observations of well-known facts prove this not to be true.

This manifest separability of goodness from good fortune, a separability so often characteristic of life in this world, later prompted Emmanuel Kant to affirm the existence of a just God and a retributive afterlife as "moral postulates" demanded by the very structure of reason. Man's innate sense that goodness and good fortune *should* go together, Kant reasoned, is an instinct that demands some future adjudication.

JOB 25

ॐ

JOB'S RESPONSES TO HIS CRITICS have had their effect, because these three appear to have become dispirited. They have reached the end of their limited intellectual resources. After the present brief rambles of Bildad, Job will hold forth without challenge until the end of chapter 31.

From the present chapter it is clear that Bildad the Shuhite has lost his way. As we have seen from the beginning, there was never anything very original about Bildad; he relied entirely on what his elders had taught him. Indeed, he made this trait his explicit boast to Job (cf. 8:8).

When we come to Bildad now, however, he does not seem to know *what* he thinks. One commentator, in fact, describes his speech as "short and out of keeping with his previous utterances."

As the chapter begins, one has the impression that we are interrupting a line of thought already in process, as though somehow we are suddenly made privy to some secret musing of Bildad's that we just happen to overhear.

Most of what Bildad says here is, in truth, simply a quotation from earlier discourses of Eliphaz (compare verses 4–6 with 4:17 and 15:14). Perhaps those words of Eliphaz had made a deep impression on Bildad. He is mumbling something that Eliphaz said earlier. He has no response at all to Job's recent argument.

Anyway, when Bildad considers that man is only a worm (verse 6), this very thought apparently prompts him to be silent, for the speech ends abruptly, and we still wonder where his thought was leading him. Bildad does not seem to know.

This sudden disorientation by Bildad, along with the lack of any third discourse by Zophar, has prompted some biblical scholars to propose various reconstructions of the text at this point.

This futile and subjective exercise is not necessary, because the text as it stands is perfectly intelligible. The dramatic loss of direction on the part of Job's critics shows simply that they have become undone. They have nothing left to say. Job has bested their best efforts. There is nothing further to add. Chapter 25 is the place where the earlier eloquence of Job's critics ends with a whimper.

Perhaps there is an added significance in the fact that their efforts end with Bildad, who has been, more than any of them, the spokesman for a certain philosophical tradition. It is the tradition itself that is breaking down under the onslaught of Job's intense, impassioned queries, so Bildad is the last of them to speak, and he has almost nothing to say.

JOB 26

૱

BILDAD HAS NOT SAID ANYTHING WORTH ANSWERING, so Job doesn't answer him. Instead, he discourses on the immense majesty of God in the phenomena of heaven and earth.

This is a further and significant development in Job's spiritual maturation through the course of the book. Especially since his avowal of personal faith in his "Redeemer" in chapter 19, Job has become more preoccupied with the world around him than with the misery of his own existence. Now he contemplates what God has made. Job's mind escapes, in this way, the confinement of his own suffering.

In the opening of the chapter, Job throws one final taunt at those who pretended to be his comforters. Just what have they accomplished (verses 2–4)?

Then he proceeds to consider the wonders of all creation, beginning with the world that has so often preoccupied him, the nether world—*sheol* and *'abaddon* (verse 6), the realm of the dead. The juxtaposition of these two words is also found in Proverbs 15:11 and 27:20.

In the present passage, the word *'abaddon* (often translated as "destruction," as in Job 31:12) serves as a personification of death itself, which seems also to be the case in Job 28:22. This is likewise how the same word is used in Revelation 9:11, where it refers to "the angel of the bottomless pit."

Though this region of the dead lies concealed from the sight of man, it is open to the eyes of God. For Job this truth is important, certainly, because his great fear, through much of this book, is that he will die and simply disappear from the gaze of God.

From his consideration of the world beneath, Job then rises to contemplate the heavens above. The "north" (*saphon*) of verse 7 refers to the lights of the northern sky, dominated by the pole star. The rendering of the canonical Greek text here, *borea*, may evoke in some readers a memory of the Northern Lights, the *aurora borealis*.

Once again, Job's juxtaposition of the nether world and the celestial world, in both of which places God is present and knowing, puts the reader in mind of Psalm 139(138), where the Psalmist exclaims, "If I ascend into heaven, You are there; If I make my bed in hell (*sheol*), behold, You are there."

These lights in the heavens, says Job, are suspended over "emptiness," *tohu* (verse 7; cf. Genesis 1:2). The earth floats beneath this emptiness above and mere "air" beneath. (This last noun, *belima*, which is found nowhere else in the Hebrew Bible, I have translated as "air," because in rabbinical literature it bears the meaning of "upper atmosphere." The canonical Greek text here, followed by several modern translations, says "nothing," *ouden*.) Since many ancient texts, including the Bible, speak of the earth as suspended "upon the waters," the imagery here in Job is doubly striking.

From air, Job moves on to consider water, first in its atmospheric form—clouds and vapors (verses 8–9), and then in its earthly form—liquid (verse 10). The shaking of the "pillars of heaven" (verse 11) suggests a booming storm. God adorns these heavens by His Spirit, *Ruach* (verse 13), a theological truth proclaimed also in Psalm 33(32):6. This is still descriptive of a storm scene, as is the "thunder of His might" in verse 14.

JOB 27

⁂

DURING THE PAST SEVERAL CHAPTERS, Job has been gaining a grip on his soul. His deep critique of the moral philosophies of his opponents has led him to neither skepticism nor despair. On the contrary, in this chapter we find him resolved to maintain the moral integrity that he displayed at the beginning of the book. Indeed, in his vow to do so, Job invokes the very God who has tried him so severely (verses 2–3).

As long as he lives, therefore, as long as "my breath [*nishmati*] is in me, And the breath of God in my nostrils [*b'aphi*]," Job will not use that breath, given by God, to "speak wickedness" (verse 4). Custody over his speech represents man's most elementary stewardship, because breath itself is the first gift that man receives from God. Job's reference to Adam's reception of this initial gift seems pretty clear in the wording of the text: "And the LORD God formed man of the dust of the ground, and breathed into his nostrils [*b'aphyo*] the breath [*nishmat*] of life; and man became a living being" (Genesis 2:7). (Elihu the Buzite will also cite this text from Genesis in Job 33:4.)

Whatever the cost, then, Job is determined to maintain this elementary stewardship of his moral life, no matter how painful, humiliating, and short that life may be (verses 5–6). All Job has left is his integrity, and he will wager everything on it. Job does not pretend to understand the moral structure of the world, as he has so often confessed. He does perceive, however, the difference between right and wrong, and he intends to live on the basis of that elementary perception.

If Job is right, though, then his critics are wrong (verse 7), so the judgment of God is inevitable in their case as well (verses 8–10). Like Socrates at his trial, Job is persuaded that God too knows the difference between a just man and an unjust man, so his unjust critics must beware. Job prepares, then, to lecture his three friends (verse 11) on the theme of the divine wisdom. (This lecture will be chapter 28.)

Often men do not seek wisdom, being distracted by the love of wealth (verses 16–17). The initial steps toward wisdom lie in the consideration of the divine judgment that hangs over human life (verses 18–23).

Psalm 49(48) may profitably be read with the second half of the present chapter of Job (verses 13–23). Both texts deal with the same theme and the same metaphysical problem, and in both of them the wisdom tradition of the Bible appeals to a universal theme of philosophy, mankind's perennial quest for understanding. Neither text refers to God's special revelation to the chosen people. No appeal is made to the divine words spoken on Sinai or to the prophets. What we find in these two texts, rather, is the God-inspired thought of biblical man addressing the human mind on its own terms. Both passages treat of the universal mortality of men, "all the inhabitants of the world, both low and high, rich and poor together." Psalm 49, based on a strictly philosophical motif, mentions God only twice, and the second of these instances sounds the very note that Job has pursued: "God will deliver my soul from the power of the grave."

JOB 28

ॐ

JOB GOES ON NOW TO MEDITATE on the sheer inaccessibility of God's secret designs, which lie concealed from human view.

In the previous chapter Job had considered the moral effects of money, or silver, on the conscience of man (27:16–17), but now he alters the sense and direction of the metaphor. These concealed wonders of the divine mind, he reflects, are more secret than veins of silver and other metals that lie buried in the bowels of the earth.

Because wisdom, like the lode veins of metals and nuggets of precious stone, lies concealed beneath the empirical surface of reality, man must dig for it. It is not available to him on the earth's surface, the place where he earns his daily bread (verse 5). When he endeavors to dig deeper, nonetheless, man discovers that the divine secrets lie further than his thought can hope to penetrate. God by His hidden wisdom made the world and continues to sustain it in existence. Wisdom rests at the very base of things, lying deeper than any precious metal or costly stone, and its worth is incomparably greater. Wisdom is buried, in fact, in the depths of God.

Job's metaphor is strengthened by the remoteness from which these various metals must be brought. Gold comes from far-off Ophir (identified as Supara in India by Josephus, *Antiquities* 8.6.4, §164; cf. the Septuagint of 2 Chronicles 8:18) and Sheba in southern Arabia. The topaz comes from Ethiopia, equally far away (verse 19). Iron and copper are imported from Cyprus (the very name of which island gives us the root of "copper" itself). Pearls and coral are raised from the depths of the sea (verse 18).

We observe that Job is no longer answering his critics in this text. He has abandoned them to their shallow theories about how the world is constructed. Job pursues, rather, the mind of God, realizing even in his pursuit that the divine wisdom vastly transcends the mind and comprehension of man.

Only God knows the way to wisdom (verse 23). God gives to man only "the *beginning* of wisdom," not its final meaning, and this beginning consists in "the fear of the Lord" (verse 28). By God's gift man can make a start in his search for wisdom, and he does so by turning away from evil. This path of conversion, or "turning away," is Job's own chosen way, and it has been since the beginning of the book (1:8; 2:3).

Job cannot read the mind of God, then, not even in those matters that concern his own life and destiny; but he does know what God requires of him, and he has affirmed already his resolve to live in perfect integrity (cf. 27:4–7). That is to say, although Job is not given to share in the secret designs of history, even his own history, he does know what is expected of him, and this is sufficient. Like those Levites charged to bear the Ark without looking into it, Job must carry forward the divine wisdom in the plodding path of his life, even if he must do this in relative darkness.

For the rest, Job's mind may quietly acquiesce in the evidence of divine wisdom revealed in the established structure of the world. Whatever else may be said about the formation of the elements, they display order and understanding, not chaos (verses 23–27).

JOB 29

୬ⁿ

THESE NEXT THREE CHAPTERS CONTAIN THE LONGEST of Job's soliloquies, in the course of which he surveys, for the last time, the overwhelming tragedy that has befallen him and the great moral puzzle that it poses to his mind. He first reviews in some detail the happiness of his former life (chapter 29), then his subsequent misery (chapter 30), and finally his own innocence throughout the trial (chapter 31).

The present chapter, then, is about "the way things used to be," those former days when Job was content, wealthy, and universally honored. Job enjoyed prosperity in those days. His lot was like that of the patriarchs in Genesis, notably Jacob. God's protecting presence was tangible in those bygone times.

Those were the days in which Job was conscious of God's protection: "God watched over me" (verse 2). The reader here recalls that Satan had made that very point with respect to Job when he told the Lord, "Have you not made a hedge around him, around his household, and around all that he has on every side?" (1:10). Job enjoyed, in those days, what the Psalmist promised: "As the mountains surround Jerusalem, / So the Lord surrounds His people / From this time forth and forever" (Psalm 125[126]:10).

Bildad earlier taunted Job, "The light is dark in his tent, / And his lamp beside him is put out" (18:10), but Job can recall the days when "His lamp shone upon my head, / And *when* by His light I walked *through* darkness" (verse 3).

Job previously enjoyed the blessings that the wisdom tradition, notably the Book of Proverbs, promises to God's loyal servants. Proverbs affirms of the Lord, "His secret counsel [*sod*] is with the upright" (3:32), and Job remembers those times, "When the friendly counsel [*sod*] of God was over my tent" (verse 4).

Respecting his relationships with his fellow men, Job was held in high esteem by everyone back then (verses 7–11, 21–23), not only because of his wealth, but also because of his righteousness and charity (verses 12–17). Contrary to the accusation of Eliphaz (22:6–9), Job was well known for his sense of justice (verse 11).

Job expected, moreover, to die in that state of universal approbation (verse 18), beloved of God and men. In those bygone days all these things seemed normal to Job, who related such blessings to his friendship with God and his doing of God's will. But then, with no discernible explanation, everything changed all at once, and this change in Job's fortunes is the subject of the next chapter.

What Job has established in the present chapter is that God formerly treated him as a just man, bestowing on him all the blessings that ancient wisdom had promised to just men.

JOB 30

THE MOTIF OF THE PRESENT CHAPTER, which is an extended and detailed contrast with Job's earlier state as described in the previous chapter, is indicated by the repeated expression, "but now" (verses 1, 9, 16). This "but now" stands in contrast to Job's "months of old" (29:2).

The thematic development of this chapter is the opposite of that in the chapter preceding. Whereas in chapter 29 Job began with his relationship to God (29:1–6) and then went on to speak of his relationship to his fellow men (29:7–25), in the present chapter he reverses the order, commencing with his alienation from his fellow men (verses 1–10) and then going to his sense of alienation from God (verses 11–31).

Formerly revered by elders, princes, and nobles (29:8–10), Job now finds himself contemned and reviled by utter nobodies. These have mocked him (verse 1) and treated him with obloquy (verses 9–10).

Never before in this book has Job been so harsh against his critics, even throwing back in their faces their low social standing. As we have seen, these three critics were men of the desert. Eliphaz came from Teman in the Negev, Zophar from Arabia, and Bildad from the far side of the Fertile Crescent. Now Job, in no little bitterness of soul, ridicules them as outlanders from the stark wilderness, "desolate and waste. . . . They had to live in the clefts of the valleys, / In caves of the earth and the rocks. / Among the bushes they brayed, / Under the nettles they nested" (verses 3, 6, 7). These are rough comments but hardly unique in the history of religious and critical thought. For example, Thomas Aquinas later described the people in that part of the world as "bestial men dwelling in deserts," "*homines bestiales in desertis morantes*" (*Summa Contra Gentiles* 1.6). If Job permits himself to be carried away somewhat at this point, we recall that he has, after all, been sorely tried by his critics.

All such treatment might be bearable from others, claims Job, but not from God (verses 16–19). In his supposed rejection by God, Job feels that his soul has been "poured out" (verse 16; cf. 10:1), an expression reminiscent of the Psalmist when he speaks of the Lord's Passion (Psalms 22[21]:15–16).

Then, abruptly, Job stops speaking about God and turns to address the Lord directly (verse 20), for the first time since 17:3. In sentiments that form a counterpart to the previous chapter (29:2–4), Job accuses God of cruelty and persecution (verse 21), but most especially of remaining silent (verse 20).

We must note here that Job does not ask to be restored to his former state. He simply wants to know why he is being so treated, since he has never treated anyone as badly as both God and man are currently treating him (verses 24–25). He does not deserve this, Job avows, and he wonders why.

JOB 31

⊰℘

We readers have known, since the beginning of the book, that Job is on trial. Indeed, this is the indispensable key to understanding the story. (For this reason, those modern critics who regard the first two chapters of Job as a later addition to the text find themselves interpreting a completely different book from the Book of Job.) The trial of Job is the major premise of this work.

This trial of Job has a clear parallel in Zechariah 3:2–6, where Satan brings accusation against the High Priest Joshua. We observe there, as here, that God is on the side of the one accused. In that passage the Lord rebukes Satan and, as a sign of Joshua's acquittal, commands that the High Priest be clothed with clean garments. Moreover, in Zechariah 6:11–14 "crowns" (yes, plural, *'ataroth*) are prepared for Joshua, to indicate his innocence. Curiously, in the present chapter Job also speaks of "crowns" (again plural, *'ataroth*) with which he will be adorned (verse 36).

Job does not seem to know, at first, that he is being tried in accord with God's own will. We even sense that Job's mind would be greatly relieved if he knew that he was being tested. Indeed, how reassured Job would be if he were aware of God's own assessment of him to Satan!

The notion of a trial has been imposed on Job's mind, not by the misfortunes that he has suffered, but by the steady flow of accusations brought against him by these three friends of his. They had originally arrived to be his "comforters," but they very quickly became his accusers. Over and over, without a shred of empirical evidence against Job, they have accused him of dreadful crimes.

If Job feels himself to be on trial, therefore, it is hard to blame him for it. Now that his three witnesses have already borne their testimony against him (more as "character witnesses" than as "eyewitnesses," to be sure), it appears now that "the prosecution rests its case" in Job's regard.

But this is all absurd, thinks Job. Even before the trial started, he had already been sentenced. In fact, the sentence is even now being executed! Everything is proceeding backwards. This is chaos! (For a strikingly similar sensation of a legal trial as an outright nightmare, an outlandish exercise in anarchy, one may profitably read Franz Kafka's *Der Prozess* or *The Trial*.)

No matter, says Job, his defense will be made, no matter what. So he "swears himself in" and proceeds with a detailed testimony to his own innocence. Job runs through a fairly high code of ethics (not unlike that of Ezekiel 18:5–9) and rings the changes on his "not guilty" plea, giving specific rebuttal to the slanderous testimony of his accusers (notably Eliphaz in chapter 22).

In this defense Job repeatedly employs the normal Hebrew formula for a legal oath or imprecation: "If I have done such-and-such, may the Lord do this-and-that to me." Often, in this formula, only the antecedent, not the consequent, is actually spoken, implying that the person swears that the accusation against him is untrue. Job employs both the complete and the truncated form of this oath rather frequently in this chapter (verses 5, 7, 9, 13, 16, 19, 20, 21, 24, 25, 26, 29, 31, 33, 38, 39). Thus, this entire chapter is just a series of imprecations, at the end of which "the words of Job are ended" (verse 40).

Is Job correct and proper in all these affirmations and denials? Does his defense actually prove Job to be innocent? In the sight of men arguably so, but not in the eyes of God. Man cannot litigate against God. In this chapter, then, Job has clearly gone too far in his claims, and the book's next speaker, Elihu the Buzite, is going to call him on it. In the book's final chapter, moreover, Job will very explicitly retract this defense.

JOB 32

❧

By the end of chapter 31, Job has answered all of the objections and arguments made by his three friends, thereby reducing them to silence. The final verse of chapter 31 suggests that "the defense rests": "The words of Job are ended." In the trial of Job, it would now seem time for a verdict.

But then, out of nowhere, an entirely new speaker suddenly bursts on the scene, an *amicus curiae* as it were, "Elihu the son of Barachel the Buzite, of the family of Ram," who rushes forth with all the impetuosity of youth. Elihu has been so silent hitherto that not even the narrator seems to have known he was present! Now, however, the young man insists on adding his own comments. Maintaining silence hitherto, he says, and thereby showing proper deference to the four older men (verse 4), this Elihu has been listening to the give-and-take of their lengthy discussion, a seemingly interminable debate that has lasted through twenty-nine chapters.

Outwardly patient during that prolonged discussion, Elihu has been inwardly seething with rancor at both Job and the other three gentlemen (verses 2–3). Hardly able to contain himself any longer, he disagrees with nearly everything said so far. Now, therefore, with a great display of indignation Elihu begins his discourse, which will run on for the next seven chapters, easily the longest single speech in the book.

Elihu begins by informing these four older men how patient he has remained during their pointless and frustrating arguments. Nonetheless, even as he boasts about his heroic longsuffering, we note the irony that Elihu mentions his own anger four times in five consecutive verses! Maybe he is not as patient as he thinks.

Job's three comforters, having exhausted their case against him, seem content now to leave the suffering Job to God, having nothing more to say. Not so Elihu. In a torrent he will vent the pressure that has been building up within him (verses 18–20).

However, even as he answers his elders, Elihu not surprisingly demonstrates the self-consciousness of youth and inexperience. He must justify himself by explaining that he is a plainspoken man, a fellow both candid and proud of it (verses 21–22).

The amusement that young, impetuous Elihu's appearance provokes in us readers should not cause us to overlook the importance of his specific contribution to the Book of Job. After all, Job has now reduced his three critics to silence. Especially in the previous three chapters, he has abundantly answered their accusations with an able defense. In some sense it would appear that Job has won his case. "Here is my mark," he proclaimed (31:35). Repeatedly in the previous chapter he has sworn to his innocence.

But has Job really demonstrated his right to hurl down a gauntlet to the Almighty? Can anyone, in fact, rightly establish such a claim? From a theological perspective it is imperative that Job now be challenged on this point, and it will be the responsibility of Elihu to do it. Elihu's contribution to the discussion, therefore, is of the essence. Without the words of Elihu, the Book of Job would be a different book. Elihu's "summing up" prepares for the divine verdict on which the book will end.

JOB 33

LIKE THE OTHER COMPONENTS in the complex discussions of the Book of Job, Elihu's contribution is a critique, not a final answer. For him the overriding discussion is not reducible to an either/or. Elihu disagrees with and criticizes both Job *and* the three comforters. The present chapter is directed to Job. The latter, says Elihu, has gone too far in his demands for a trial between himself and God. Elihu confronts him on the point (verse 5).

Job's three friends remained aloof from him, assuming a morally superior attitude. Elihu will do no such thing. He confesses himself at one with Job in their human solidarity, their descent from Adam (verses 4, 6). He will not talk down to Job as the comforters have.

That matter established, Elihu begins by summarizing Job's protestations of innocence (verses 9–11), a claim advanced repeatedly throughout the book (cf. 9:21; 10:7; 13:18, 24, 27; 23:10; 27:5–6; 31 *passim*). This claim is pretentious, says Elihu, because "God is greater than man" (verse 12). That is to say, God owes man no explanations at all (verses 13–14), nor will Elihu attempt to act as God's defender.

Then, like Eliphaz near the beginning (4:12–15), Elihu refers to dreams (verse 15), presumably the nightmares of Job himself (7:14). Such dreams, Elihu asserts, are providential. God employs them to draw men back from rash, dangerous, and unwarranted decisions (verses 16–17).

Elihu, displaying a compassion absent in the comments of Job's three comforters, suggests that Job may have failed to recognize the true significance of his nightmares. Perhaps God intended them to pull him back from a reckless path.

The parallel between the dream of Eliphaz, Job's first interlocutor, and the dreams mentioned by Elihu is not accidental. There is a deliberate correspondence between them and a contrast. Both men, in answering Job, start with dreams, but we are struck by a great difference of tone between the two. Eliphaz appealed to his own dream as the point of departure for establishing a moral judgment on Job. Elihu does not. He suggests to Job, rather, that his dream may have been the voice of

God speaking to him in concern and warning. That is to say, Job's nightmare, far from indicating God's absence from his life, may have indicated the very opposite.

This approach will be operative in all of Elihu's discourse. The three friends have understood Job's sufferings to be simply punishments. Is there no other rational explanation? asks Elihu. Why presume that all suffering is by way of punishment?

Before putting that question to the three friends, Elihu first puts it to Job. Why not consider that these terrible sufferings, of which Job has so bitterly complained, represent God's effort to preserve Job from the powers of death and darkness (verses 22–30)? Why not regard them, in fact, as a "chastening" (verse 19)? That is to say, is it really so obvious that suffering is always a punishment?

We readers, of course, instructed by the first two chapters of the book, are aware that Elihu is much closer to the correct answer than anyone who has spoken hitherto.

JOB 34

❧

ELIHU, HAVING ADDRESSED JOB, turns now to the other three characters in the story. These have not, Elihu believes, answered Job's challenges to God in a proper way. That is to say, Job's friends have made an inadequate presentation of the traditional wisdom itself.

Elihu's remarks to Job's critics are among the book's best parts, variations of which will appear in God's own account near the end. Elihu's comments are heavily didactic, nonetheless, and seldom rise to the high poetic levels of the other speakers, especially Job himself.

Elihu's chief objection to Job's friends concerns their exclusive attribution of divine punishment to human suffering. Punishment and reward, Elihu argues, do not comprise between them the whole of God's dealing with man. There is another and important aspect to the "negative side of God," namely, divine correction and exhortation. God, says Elihu, is correcting and exhorting Job by permitting his sufferings.

We now meet explicitly for the first time (except in the introductory chapters in this book) a new thesis: God sends afflictions not only to punish, but also to admonish. If a man accepts these sufferings as God's loving correction and invitation, rather than as a punishment, he will avoid the pride and self-satisfaction that may sometimes be the peril of a godly life. Such God-sent afflictions will serve, therefore, as a restorative. Neither Job nor any of his friends, Elihu believes, has sufficiently considered this perspective.

In order to advance this argument, however, Elihu must put to rest any notion of injustice in God. Such an idea involves an internal contradiction, Elihu contends (verses 10, 12); the very existence of the world depends on the thesis of God's righteousness (verses 13–15).

There is no justice higher than God (verse 17), nor is the Almighty likely to be influenced by the more powerful of His creatures (verse 19). Truly, nothing in man's experience is hidden from the gaze of God (verses 21–22). The font and source of justice, God holds all human activity to the same standard and the same sanctions (verses 24–28).

What Job's comforters should have asserted is that God, through the sufferings that He has sent to Job, had only the latter's proper correction in mind (verses 31–32). The insistence of his friends, however, that Job was being justly punished for his crimes simply provoked him to an improper assertion of his innocence. It was the responsibility of these men, says Elihu, to provide Job with proper instruction. The ineptitude of their arguments has served only to incite the sufferer into open rebellion against the Almighty (verses 35–37).

Moreover, Job's call for a trial, in which he might argue his case against God, distorts the proper relationship between God and man. God is not man's enemy or opponent. God needs opponents no more than He needs powerful friends, nor does He ever act from a sense of need.

JOB 35

❧

HAVING ADDRESSED JOB'S COMPANIONS, Elihu turns again to Job himself and gives a fair paraphrase of Job's position. Do not some of Job's comments suggest that he thinks himself more righteous than God (verse 2)? Job may not have made so outlandish a claim in so many words, but what he has said amounts to the same thing (verse 3; cf. 4:17; 13:18; 15:3; 19:6–7; 21:15; 27:2–6). Now, asks Elihu, is this at all likely?

He turns Job's gaze upwards, then, to the physical symbols of God's transcendence, the clouds above his head (verse 5). God is not, in Himself, altered by either man's virtue or his vice (verses 6–9). God does what He does, simply because He is free and righteous. He is not more or less righteous or free because of anything man does. How, after all, can human behavior touch God?

Is Elihu's own presentation of the question entirely adequate, nonetheless? While there is a sense in which God is not, in Himself, affected by either man's virtue or his vice, this is hardly a sufficient statement of the case. It is certainly not true that God is indifferent to man's state, and the full context of Elihu's comments show that he knows this very well.

Rather, the point Elihu has in mind to make in this chapter is that no one has a forensic claim on God; indeed, even to voice such a claim is, in some measure, to attempt to put oneself on God's level. This, says Elihu, is what Job has done.

Is God indifferent to human suffering, or does He reject the cries of those in pain? No, but this does not mean that such cries are, in every case, really worthy of a hearing. Sometimes such pleadings are accompanied by the beating of a sinful heart (verses 12–13). Elihu's point here is that not once has Job pleaded for forgiveness. His prayer has lacked humility. God hears man's prayer because He is merciful, not because man deserves to be heard. If God seems to disregard Job's prayer at the present, then, may it not be the case that there is still something wrong with Job's prayer?

Job's real trial, in fact, his true "temptation," does not come from

God. "God cannot be tempted by evil, nor does He Himself tempt anyone. But each one is tempted when he is drawn away by his own desires and enticed" (James 1:13–14). The trial endured by Job has demonstrated, not that Job has deserved to suffer what he has been obliged to suffer, but that, in spite of this fact, all is not well with Job. This painful trial has shown that Job himself is not beyond improvement. His prayer has made it evident that Job does not yet love God for God's own sake.

Job's pain has prompted him to argue that God both ignores the wickedness of evil men and neglects to reward just men (21:7–21). These are foolish words, retorts Elihu (verse 16). God has His own way of taking care of such matters, and things are not always as they appear, either with respect to God or with respect to ourselves.

God has not in anger punished Job for his words, nonetheless, and He has overlooked the foolishness of Job's rebellious comments (verse 15). Job must now show the same patience that God has demonstrated. Job has complained that he does not see God, but Elihu insists that he must wait for God (verse 14).

JOB 36

ॐ

ELIHU FINISHED THE PREVIOUS CHAPTER by accusing Job of *hebel*, variously translated as "vanity" (cf. KJV "in vain") and "emptiness" (cf. RSV "empty talk"). This word, so important to the Book of Ecclesiastes (where it appears 38 times, most famously in "vanity of vanities, and all is vanity"), puts a compelling finger on the problem. In the Book of Job (unlike the Book of Ecclesiastes), the problem of *hebel* is not an alleged emptiness in the universe (though Job in 7:16 does momentarily wonder about this); indeed, almost all the speakers in Job explicitly refute this notion of a chaotic world.

What is at issue in Job is, rather, whether or not man's moral life will be *hebel*. Will Job himself prove to be only vanity and emptiness by his choices? There is irony in Elihu's comment here, because *hebel* is the very word Job earlier used to describe the "comfort" his friends were providing for him (21:34).

In the Book of Job, God's universe is in no danger. Job is the one in danger. Very serious danger. He must exercise caution, says Elihu, lest his mind be lured into total rebellion (verses 17–18).

God, says Elihu, does not hate (verse 5). Nor is He capricious; He renders judgment for the poor (verses 6, 15). When God does chastise, it is ever with a view to man's correction and repentance (verses 8–10, 22). The time of trial, therefore, is the proper occasion of taking stock of one's conscience. However, not to receive the judgment of God with repentance is most serious (verses 11–14). It is Job who may be failing in this regard, not God, and Job's present path is parlous. Let not God's chastisement lead him into rebellion.

At the end Elihu waxes poetic, and the chapter closes with his praise of God in creation (verses 26–33), praise that continues into the following chapter (37:1–13). Virtually all the lines of this paean of praise have parallels in the Book of Psalms and elsewhere in Holy Scripture.

Elihu's point is that God is always to be praised, regardless of how suffering man feels on the subject. No matter what the lesson to be learned, God is ever the Teacher (verse 22). It is not man's place to correct his Teacher (verse 23). Job is invited, therefore, to join all rational voices in the praise of God (verses 24–25).

Even from a purely psychological perspective, there is much wisdom in Elihu's admonition here. God's richest praise has ever been raised to heaven in times of suffering. Indeed, it is not a rare moment in human existence when a man's only two real choices are either to praise God or to feel sorry for himself. Elihu invites Job to learn this lesson.

The end of this chapter (along with the first verses of the next) describes a storm. To the present writer it does not seem far-fetched to think of Elihu's discourse at this point being accompanied by a real storm that he is describing while it happens.

JOB 37

ॐ

THE FIRST HALF OF THIS CHAPTER continues Elihu's praise of God. This is Elihu's way of exhorting Job, similar to the way that St. James exhorts all of us: "Is any among you suffering? Let him pray" (James 5:13). The deliberate praise of God is the proper and godly response of a faithful soul to the experience of suffering.

For example, the longsuffering Martin Rinckart in 1630 composed his well-known hymn, *Nun danket Alle Gott* ("Now thank we all our God"), as his response to the horrible trials of his native Eilenburg, which suffered from the devastating plague of 1619, several failed harvests, and the three different times the city was sacked during the Thirty Years' War. In addition, Rinckart himself suffered that year from profound domestic grief.

Moreover, the popular choice of Rinckart's stirring hymn to be sung in celebration of Thanksgiving Day reflects the attitude of those original pilgrims who first celebrated that holiday in our country. They too knew how to praise God for His mercy in the midst of adversity.

The section of Elihu's hymn of praise in this chapter dwells especially on the imagery of the storm. He finally closes his discourse by exhorting Job to dwell more on what he knows of God and to assess his own suffering in the light of that knowledge. Elihu addresses Job directly, exhorting him to weigh God's wondrous works. He puts to Job a list of parallel questions bearing on Job's own ignorance of God's ways (verses 15–18). To each of these questions, Job's only possible answer is "no." He cannot explain anything about God. Elihu then challenges Job himself to be the teacher (verses 19–20).

Most striking of Elihu's comments is that respecting the sun (verse 21). Man's inability to gaze directly at the light of heaven does not lessen the reality of that light. The inability is in man's own limited faculty, not in the truth of what he is unable to gaze upon. Yet, the real light of God is brighter than the sun. Elihu means here that primeval light, the luminosity of the created universe, called forth by God's voice on the first day of Creation, days before the sun was made (Genesis 1:3, 16). If

•

man is unable to look directly at the sun, how does he dare to attempt to look directly at that stronger light at the heart of created reality? His inability to do so in no way calls the light itself into question.

What, finally, is to be said of Elihu's contribution to this discussion about suffering and justice? It is worth remarking that his lengthy discourse prepares the way for God's revelation to Job in the book's closing chapters. It should also be noted that God does not reprimand Elihu as He does Job and the three comforters.

In the Book of Job, Elihu never arrives on the scene, nor does he leave it; he has neither beginning of days, nor end of life. Like Melchizedek, Elihu remains one of the more mysterious characters of Holy Scripture.

JOB 38

⁓

Now the Lord Himself will speak, for the first time since chapter 2. After all, Job has been *asking* for God to speak (cf. 13:22; 23:5; 30:20; 31:35), and now he will get a great deal more than he anticipated. With a mere gesture, as it were, God proceeds to brush aside all the theories and pseudoproblems of the preceding chapters.

God speaks "from the whirlwind," *min sa'arah*, an expression sometimes associated in the Bible with theophanic experience. For example, the word famously appears twice in association with Elijah's ascent in the fiery chariot (2 Kings 2:1, 11). In other examples the word emphasizes the divine judgment, particularly in the Book of Psalms (107:25, 29; 148:8) and in the prophets (Isaiah 29:6; 40:24; 41:16; Jeremiah 23:19; 30:23; Zechariah 9:14).

More especially, however, one is struck by the word in the theophanies recorded in Ezekiel, the only other Old Testament book in which the character of Job appears. Thus, the Lord manifests Himself in this way to Ezekiel in the book's inaugural vision by the banks of the Kabari Canal: "Then I looked, and behold, a whirlwind"—*sa'arah* (1:4), which the prophet then describes at some length. In the other two places where the word appears in Ezekiel, the emphasis is once again on the divine judgment (13:11, 13).

This same emphasis marks the whirlwind in Job. He has asked for a judgment from on high. Now he will hear it.

We should observe that the One who speaks from the whirlwind is "the Lord." Except when Job uses this divine name in 12:9, this is the first time it has appeared in the Book of Job since chapter 2. It is significant that the God who speaks in these closing chapters is identified with Israel's Lord. Job's critics, including Elihu, have their various theories about "God," but the only God who will address them definitively is the Lord, Israel's transcendent and living God of judgment and mercy. This is the God who lives and speaks beyond all philosophical and religious theory.

In this respect, the Lord's words to Job out of the whirlwind may be considered in the light of His words to Moses on the mountain, especially His auto-identification: "I am the LORD your God" (Exodus 20:2). This Lord speaks to Moses, if not in a whirlwind, at least just as impressively. There were, we are told, "thunderings and lightnings, and a thick cloud on the mountain." Moreover, "Mount Sinai was completely in smoke, because the LORD descended upon it in fire. Its smoke ascended like the smoke of a furnace, and the whole mountain quaked greatly" (Exodus 19:16, 18). Now the Lord, the God who spoke to Moses, addresses Job.

At this point, all philosophical discussion comes to an end. There are questions, to be sure, but the questions now come from the Lord. Indeed, we observe in this chapter that God does not answer Job's earlier questions. The Lord does not so much as even notice those questions; He renders them hopelessly irrelevant. He has His own questions to put to Job.

The purpose of these questions is not merely to bewilder Job. These questions have to do, rather, with God's providence over all things. The Lord is suggesting to Job that His providence over Job's own life is even more subtle and majestic than these easier questions which God proposes and which Job cannot begin to answer, questions about the construction of the world (verses 4–15), the courses of the heavenly bodies (verses 31–38), the marvels of earth and sea (verses 16–30), and animal life (38:39—39:30). Utterly surrounded by things that he cannot understand, will Job still demand to know mysteries even more mysterious?

If the world itself contains creatures that seem improbable and bewildering to the human mind, should not man anticipate that there are even more improbable and bewildering aspects to the subtler forms of the divine providence? God will not be reduced simply to an answer to Job's shallow questions. Indeed, the divine voice from the whirlwind never once deigns even to notice Job's questions. They are implicitly subsumed into a mercy vaster and far richer.

Implicit in these questions to Job is the quiet reminder of the Lord's affectionate provision for all His creatures. If God so cares for the birds of the air and the plants of the fields, how much more for Job!

JOB 39

ॐ

THE LORD, HAVING SURVEYED FOR JOB'S BENEFIT the myriad manifestations of divine wisdom and power in the realms of astronomy, physics, and botany, now (beginning in 38:39) starts to examine the world of zoology.

Several animals are considered in varying degrees of detail: the lion and the raven, both of which, powerful hunters though they be, depend on God's provision (38:39–41); the mountain goat (or ibex), the deer, and the wild ass, all characterized by the freedom of their migrations (verses 1–8); the *rîmu*, a now extinct species of ox that man never managed to tame (verses 9–12; the Vulgate has "rhinoceros"); the ostrich, renowned for both its stupidity and its speed, and evidently placed here (verses 13–18) to be in proximity to the next animal; the mighty war charger, whose neck, larger than its head, is "clothed with thunder," and who revels to be once again in the excitement of battle (verses 19–25); and finally the hawk and the eagle, accomplished hunters who see from afar (verses 26–30).

The greatest detail is devoted to the only domesticated animal in the list, the destrier, or warhorse. The horse in antiquity was reserved for combat. It was not used for plowing (the work of the ox), nor for carrying burdens (the work of donkeys), nor for ordinary riding (the work of mules and donkeys). The horse, this most noble and impressive of all the animals that man has tamed, was employed exclusively for battle. Originally, equestrian warfare was by chariots, but fighting from horseback was introduced by at least the seventh century B.C. This latter case is what the Book of Job seems to have in mind, since the text does not mention chariots.

In the case of the ostrich there are special ironies relished for their sheer humor. This proud, strutting bird (verse 13) shows that she is not really very bright (verse 17). Indeed, she does not have enough sense even to protect her eggs adequately (verses 14–16). Here the Book of Job shares the common ancient view that the ostrich was lacking in elementary intelligence. Seneca testified that calling someone an ostrich was the most severe of insults, and Diodorus of Sicily humorously suggested that the ostrich hid its head in the sand to protect its weakest part. Yet, when it comes to speed, says the Lord to Job, this otherwise unimpressive ostrich has no equal (verse 18).

Such a listing of animals and their habits, described for the purpose of praising God, is found likewise in Psalm 104 (103), the common introductory psalm of Vespers. It speaks of donkeys, birds, cattle, storks, wild goats, rock badgers, and lions. Similarly, Psalm 147 portrays the raven and the horse. When animals are described in the Book of Proverbs, on the other hand, it is normally for the purpose of drawing some moral lesson.

The point driven home in the illustrations in this chapter of Job is that all these animals, even the warhorse, have an existence quite independent of man. God made them the way they are, and they tend not to answer to human expectations. Does this not show that man is bewildered even by things that are beneath him? How much more, therefore, must he humble his mind before mysteries above him!

JOB 40

ॐ

THIS CHAPTER, UNLIKE THE TWO PRECEDING, permits Job to put in a word of his own. He uses the occasion simply to confess his vileness and to state his resolve to remain silent before the Lord (verses 3–5), sentiments that will be expanded in the book's final chapter.

Job has no plans to debate God. He will say nothing further. His earlier aspirations have really been answered, after all, because God has now spoken, and this is essentially what Job had sought. God continues, then.

As the two preceding chapters dealt with the mysteries of God's activity in the realm of nature, the first part of this chapter turns to God's presence in the order of conscience (verses 8–14). If Job understood next to nothing about the first, he knows even less about the second.

This revelation, too, comes *min sa'arah*, "from the whirlwind" (verse 6; 38:1). Once again, as well, Job is commanded to gird up his loins like a man (verse 7; 38:3). Job is queried about who, on the evidence, is more righteous, himself or God (verse 8)? Does Job really desire a forensic setting to determine this question? Is Job capable of dealing with the myriad moral dilemmas involved in every man's life, as God must do (verses 9–14)? In short, Job is trapped in his own subjectivity, unable to see the world from God's perspective. There is no place where he may stand to indict the Lord.

Then, dramatically, the divine discourse goes from the realm of ethics and conscience to a consideration of two symbols of apparent chaos, both of them fearsome and incomprehensible: behemoth and Leviathan.

Although "behemoth" is simply the plural of the Hebrew word for "beast" or "animal," its description here seems largely to be drawn from the hippopotamus (*hippos* = "horse" and *potamos* = "river"—so "river horse"), huge, strong, invincible, even unchallenged, rightly afraid of nothing (verses 15–24). Other commentators have variously argued that the behemoth is really the crocodile, or a wild ox-buffalo, or some other kind of wild bull.

This is one of those questions that it is important *not* to decide. The reason for this has to do with the symbolic value of the description. The behemoth, though portrayed with features recognized in animals already well known, represents simply "the beast." This is the general sense that the Hebrew plural form "behemoth" has in several places in Holy Scripture (cf. Psalms 8:7; 49[48]:10; 73[72]:22; Joel 1:20; 2:22; Habakkuk 2:17).

That is to say, this behemoth is a great deal more than any particular beast. It represents, rather, the wildness of untamed animal existence. It conveys in symbolism the truth that the world is not made according to man's own measure. This Beast is irrational in the sense that it does not make rational choices. Yet, its behavior is not irrational, not chaotic, because it obeys the integral instincts placed in it by its Creator. It is not tame, but it is not really chaotic. In its own way, it declares the glory of God.

JOB 41

꒳

THE SECOND BEAST, LEVIATHAN, is a water monster mentioned elsewhere in Holy Scripture (Psalms 74:14; Isaiah 27:1). Although it represents any sort of sea monster (sharks, for instance), its description here seems to be drawn largely from the crocodile. This latter animal obviously served as a chief model for the classical picture of the idealized fearsome dragon—the Dragon of all dragons, as it were—because of its very large mouth (resembling, in this respect, the hippopotamus), its many sharp teeth, its impregnable hide, and a tail so large and powerful that one can easily imagine it knocking down the very stars in heaven (cf. Revelation 12:4). Only a little imagination is required to think of this creature as breathing fire (verses 19–21). Leviathan, in short, makes for man a rather unsatisfactory pet (verses 4–5) and an even worse conversationalist (verse 3).

All of this goes to say that man cannot domesticate Leviathan. He is resistant to all human efforts to control him and thus remains in this world the symbol of everything in existence that is recalcitrant to man's ability, especially his rational ability, to take it in hand.

It is worth remarking that, just as the Book of Job links the behemoth and Leviathan in this section, we know from Herodotus and Pliny that Egyptian traditions tended to pair the hippopotamus and the crocodile as two most dangerous animals.

But there is another consideration here as well. Both behemoth and Leviathan are God's household pets, as it were, creatures that He cares for with gentle concern, His very playmates (compare Psalms 104 [103]:26). God is pleased with them. Job cannot take the measure of these animals, but the Lord does.

What, then, do these considerations say to Job? Well, Job has been treading on some very dangerous ground through some of this book, and it is about time that he manifest a bit more deference before things he does not understand. Behemoth and Leviathan show that the endeavor to transgress the limits of human understanding is not merely futile. There is about it a strong element of danger. A man can be devoured by it.

It is remarkable that God's last narrative to Job resembles nothing so much as a fairy tale, or at least that darker part of a fairy tale that deals with dragons. Instead of pleading His case with Job, as Job has often requested, the Lord deals with him as with a child. Job must return to his childhood's sense of awe and wonder, so the Lord tells him a children's story about a couple of unimaginably dangerous dragons. These dragons, nonetheless, are only pets in the hands of God. Job is left simply with the story. It is the Lord's final word in the argument.

JOB 42

ॐ

THE TRIAL OF JOB IS OVER. This last chapter of this book contains (1) a statement of repentance by Job (verses 1–6), (2) the Lord's reprimand of Eliphaz and his companions (verses 7–8), and (3) a final narrative section, at the end of which Job begins the second half of his life (verses 9–17). The book begins and ends, then, in narrative form.

First, one observes in Job's repentance that he arrives at a new state of humility, not from a consideration of his own sins, but by an experience of God's overwhelming power and glory. (Compare Peter in Luke 5:1–8.) When God finally reveals Himself to Job, the revelation is different from anything Job either sought or expected, but clearly he is not disappointed.

All through this book, Job has been proclaiming his personal integrity, but now this consideration is not even in the picture; he has forgotten all about any alleged personal integrity. It is no longer pertinent to his relationship to God (verse 6). Job is justified by faith, not by any claims to personal integrity. All that is in the past, and Job leaves it behind.

Second, the Lord then turns and deals with the three comforters who have failed so miserably in their task. Presuming to speak for the Almighty, they have fallen woefully short of the glory of God.

Consequently, Job is appointed to be the intercessor on their behalf. Ironically, the offering that God prescribes to be made on behalf of the three comforters (verse 8) is identical to that which Job had offered for his children out of fear that they might have cursed God (1:5). The Book of Job both begins and ends, then, with Job and worship and intercession. In just two verses (7–8) the Lord four times speaks of "My servant Job," exactly as He had spoken of Job to Satan at the beginning of the book. But Job, for his part, must bear no grudge against his friends, and he is blessed by the Lord in the very act of his praying for them (verse 10).

Ezekiel, remembering Job's prayer more than his patience, listed him with Noah and Daniel, all three of whom he took to be men endowed with singular powers of intercession before the Most High (Ezekiel 14:14–20).

The divine reprimand of Job's counselors also implies that their many accusations against Job were groundless. Indeed, Job had earlier warned them of God's impending anger with them in this matter (13:7–11), and now that warning is proved accurate (verse 7). Also, ironically, whereas Job's friends fail utterly in their efforts to comfort him throughout almost the entire book, they succeed at the end (verse 11).

Third, in the closing narrative we learn that Job lives 140 years, exactly twice the normal span of a man's life (cf. Psalm 90[89]:10). Each of his first seven sons and three daughters is *replaced* at the end of the story, and all of his original livestock is exactly doubled (Job 1:3; 42:12). St. John Chrysostom catches the sense of this final section of Job:

> His sufferings were the occasion of great benefit. His substance was doubled, his reward increased, his righteousness enlarged, his crown made more lustrous, his reward more glorious. He lost his children, but he received, not those restored, but others in their place, and even those he still held in assurance unto the Resurrection (*Homilies on 2 Timothy* 7).

ABOUT THE AUTHOR

Patrick Henry Reardon is pastor of All Saints Antiochian Orthodox Church in Chicago, Illinois, and Senior Editor of *Touchstone: A Journal of Mere Christianity*.

ALSO BY PATRICK HENRY REARDON

Christ in the Psalms

A highly inspirational book of meditations on the Psalms by one of the most insightful and challenging Orthodox writers of our day. Avoiding both syrupy sentimentality and arid scholasticism, *Christ in the Psalms* takes the reader on a thought-provoking and enlightening pilgrimage through this beloved "Prayer Book" of the Church.

Which psalms were quoted most frequently in the New Testament, and how were they interpreted? How has the Church historically understood and utilized the various psalms in her liturgical life? How can we perceive the image of Christ shining through the psalms? Lively and highly devotional, thought-provoking yet warm and practical, *Christ in the Psalms* sheds a world of insight upon each psalm, and offers practical advice for how to make the Psalter a part of our daily lives. Paperback, 328 pages (ISBN 1-888212-20-9) Order No. 004927—$17.95*

Christ in His Saints

In this sequel to *Christ in the Psalms,* popular pastor, author, and scholar, Patrick Henry Reardon, once again applies his keen intellect to a topic he loves most dearly. Here he examines the lives of almost one hundred and fifty saints and heroes from the Scriptures—everyone from Abigail to Zephaniah, Adam to St. John the Theologian. This well-researched work is a veritable cornucopia of Bible personalities: Old Testament saints, New Testament saints, "Repentant saints," "Zealous saints," "Saints under pressure" . . . they're all here, and their stories are both fascinating and uplifting.

But *Christ in His Saints* is far more than just a biblical who's who. These men and women represent that ancient family into which, by baptism, all believers have been incorporated. Together they compose that great "cloud of witnesses" cheering us on and inspiring us through word and deed. Paperback, 320 pages (ISBN 1-888212-68-3) Order No. 006538—$17.95*

*plus applicable tax and postage & handling charges.
Please call Conciliar Press at 800-967-7377 for complete ordering information.

The Gospel of Mark: The Suffering Servant
by Fr. Lawrence Farley

Israel expected the Messiah to be a conquering hero who would liberate the Jews from their Roman servitude. But instead, Christ came as a suffering servant to liberate all mankind from slavery to sin. The Gospel of Mark records Christ's public ministry as a journey to the Cross, yet—paradoxically again—as a time of vigorous action when His miracles astounded the multitudes, and His boldness infuriated His foes.

Paperback, 224 pages (ISBN 1-888212-54-3) Order No. 006035—$16.95*

Romans: A Gospel for All
by Fr. Lawrence Farley

The Apostle Paul lived within a swirl of controversy. False Christians—Judaizers—dogged his every step, slandering his motives, denying his apostolic authority, and seeking to overthrow his Gospel teaching. They argued their case loudly, and Paul knew that he must give the literary performance of his life. The result was the Epistle to the Romans, in which he demonstrates the truth of his Gospel—a Gospel for all men—and thereby vindicates his apostolic authority.

Paperback, 208 pages (ISBN 1-888212-51-9) Order No. 005675—$14.95*

The Prison Epistles:
Philippians – Ephesians – Colossians – Philemon
by Fr. Lawrence Farley

From the depths of a Roman prison, words of encouragement and instruction flowed from the tongue of the great Apostle Paul. Written down by scribes, his words went forth as a series of letters to Christian communities throughout the Roman Empire. The Apostle Paul may have been fettered and shackled to a series of Roman guards, but the Word he preached remained unfettered and free.

Contains commentaries on the epistles to the Philippians, Ephesians, Colossians, and Philemon—which were written while the Apostle Paul was in prison.

Paperback, 224 pages (ISBN 1-888212-52-7) Order No. 006034—$15.95*

THE ORTHODOX STUDY BIBLE:
New Testament and Psalms

An edition of the New Testament and Psalms that offers Bible study aids written from an Orthodox perspective. Prepared under the direction of canonical

Orthodox theologians and hierarchs, *The Orthodox Study Bible* presents a remarkable combination of historic theological insights and practical instruction in Christian living. *The Orthodox Study Bible* also provides a personal guide to help you apply biblical truths to your daily life with such excellent aids as: carefully prepared study notes on the text; a chart of Scripture readings to offer guidance for daily devotions; a guide for morning and evening prayers; readings for feast days; quotations from early Church Fathers such as St. John Chrysostom, St. Ignatius of Antioch, St. Gregory of Nyssa, and St. Athanasius; a glossary of Orthodox Christian terminology; and the New King James Version translation with center-column cross references and translation notes.

Genuine Leather Edition—$49.95*; Hardcover Edition—$29.95*;
Paperback Edition—$23.95*

Journey to the Kingdom: Reflections on the Sunday Gospels
by Fr. John Mack

Reflections on selected Sunday Gospel readings. Father John's insights into familiar Bible passages that we have often heard, but may not truly have understood, are excellent. He takes us through the highlights of the church year and lovingly opens up the Gospel stories to us with patristic and biblical wisdom. Many of the reflections are filled with stories of the saints, as well as observations about living in the twenty-first century that lead us to ask deeper questions about our own lives. *Journey to the Kingdom* deals with sin and grace, repentance and confession, living by faith, and many other needful topics.

Paperback, 208 pages (ISBN 1-888212-27-6) Order No. 005132—$13.95*

Sola Scriptura
by Fr. John Whiteford

An Orthodox analysis of a Protestant bastion: private interpretation of Scripture. Exposes the fallacies on which this doctrine is based and explains the Orthodox approach to Holy Scripture.

47-page booklet (ISBN 1-888212-04-7) Order No. 001983—$3.95*

*plus applicable tax and postage & handling charges.
Please call Conciliar Press at 800-967-7377 for complete ordering information.